PRAYERS AND PROMISES

HOME TO HEATHER CREEK

PRAYERS and PROMISES

Robert Elmer

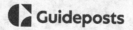

Home to Heather Creek is a trademark of Guideposts.

Copyright © 2023 by Guideposts. All rights reserved.

This book, or parts thereof, may not be reproduced, stored in a retrieval system, or transmitted in any form or by any means, electronic, mechanical, photocopying, recording, or otherwise, without the written permission of the publisher.

The characters and events in this book are fictional, and any resemblance to actual persons or events is coincidental.

Scripture references are from the following sources: *The Holy Bible, King James Version* (KJV). *The Holy Bible, New International Version* (NIV). Copyright © 1973, 1978, 1984, 2011 by Biblica, Inc. Used by permission of Zondervan. All rights reserved worldwide. www.zondervan.com

Published by Guideposts Books & Inspirational Media
100 Reserve Road, Suite E200
Danbury, CT 06810
Guideposts.org

Cover by Lookout Design, Inc.
Interior design by Cindy LaBreacht
Additional design work by Müllerhaus
Typeset by Aptara, Inc.

ISBN 978-1-959634-58-4 (hardcover)
ISBN 978-1-959634-62-1 (epub)
ISBN 978-1-959634-59-1 (epdf)

Printed in the United States of America
10 9 8 7 6 5 4 3 2 1

Acknowledgments

My father—who was born as autumn days approached Copenhagen—has always reminded me through his life's example how to "rejoice in hope, be patient in tribulation, be constant in prayer" (Romans 12:12, ESV). I can think of no better inspiration for the story of prayers and promises you're about to read.

—Robert Elmer

Home to Heather Creek

Before the Dawn

Sweet September

Circle of Grace

Homespun Harvest

A Patchwork Christmas

An Abundance of Blessings

Every Sunrise

Promise of Spring

April's Hope

Seeds of Faith

On the Right Path

Sunflower Serenade

Second Chances

Prayers and Promises

PRAYERS AND PROMISES

Chapter One

They had been married sixty-two years, almost as long as Charlotte had been alive. But today Bud Harbinger didn't recognize his wife, Greta.

Charlotte swallowed her tears and fended off her fear of ever finding herself in Greta Harbinger's difficult position. How did Greta manage? And who knew it would be so heartwrenching to volunteer a few hours a week at the Bedford Gardens Convalescent Center?

"Here we go, Mrs. Harbinger," she said. "We'll get those flowers in water for you, so everyone can enjoy them."

Charlotte stepped to the little sink of the tiny patient room and filled a clear-glass vase with water from the tap. She rearranged a couple of ferns and pinched a leaf or two, arranging the bouquet as best she could, trying to decide where it should go. Over on the window shelf, next to the framed pictures of smiling children and grandchildren, where it could catch a fading ray of autumn light? Or perhaps on the small upright dresser, already draped with a nice tablecloth decorated with counted cross-stitch images of bluebirds and creeping golden flowers?

Each personal touch contrasted with the room's pale, institutional green walls.

Little Mrs. Harbinger looked up from the Bible she had been reading to her husband, and smiled sweetly back at Charlotte, the way she always did.

"Thank you," she told Charlotte in her sweet voice, flavored with the faded but clear touch of a German accent. "I know Bud will appreciate that."

Charlotte often did this sort of thing for patients and their families. It was her job as a volunteer, after all, and the least she could do for Greta, who spent more time here with her husband than anyone else.

"This is from your son and daughter-in-law in St. Louis," explained Charlotte, pointing out the small card that had come with the flowers. "See, Mr. Harbinger? It says 'Happy Anniversary from Andy, Amy, and the kids.' That's very nice of them to remember you. And these flowers are so lovely."

She tried her best to keep her voice normal, level, and steady, just as the center's head nurse had taught her to do when she had started volunteering here. With Alzheimer's patients, it was too easy to slip into a sort of baby talk.

"They are lovely." Greta touched a carnation and smiled. "I wonder if they remember the flower story I used to tell them." She paused for a moment, as if embarrassed, and then shook her head.

"I'd like to hear it," Charlotte urged her. "Please."

"Oh, it's nothing, really. My mother just always told me that red carnations remind us that God is faithful. It was a tradition in her family."

"In Germany?"

"Actually, they were from Slovenia, to the south. My father was German."

"Well, I think that's a lovely custom to remember. Did you have flowers in your home?"

"In Strausberg just outside of Berlin, where I lived—not often, but on special occasions sometimes. The last time I saw my father . . ." She raised a hand to the collar of her white blouse as she recalled the memory. "It was at the start of the war, and he was leaving to report for duty. Of course we were all sad to see him go, and I was just a young girl, eleven or twelve years old, and crying my heart out. But I pinned a red carnation on his lapel, the way you see now at weddings. I thought perhaps it would bring him back, but . . ."

Her voice trailed off. Bud looked up from where he sat in an oversized red-vinyl recliner, confusion lining his brow. His wife had combed his shock of thin, gray hair and had straightened the collar of his pressed, white shirt.

"Who are you?" he demanded, looking suspiciously at Charlotte as she placed the mixed bouquet of roses, asters, chrysanthemums, and, of course, carnations on the windowsill next to where he spent most of his days. The waning light of a distant October sun caught the beautiful blend of reds, yellows, oranges, and violet just so, even as it began to hide behind a threatening bank of orange-tinged dark clouds to the west. The flowers smelled lovely—a welcome addition to the less pleasant scents of the convalescent home.

"You know Charlotte Stevenson." Greta's voice sounded

like a kindly kindergarten teacher's, perhaps because she had once served in that capacity at Bedford Elementary years ago. "She's been helping us here for the past few weeks."

He didn't respond, so she went on.

"She married Bob Stevenson. You know Bob. You used to work on his tractors all the time, remember?"

Charlotte felt for poor Greta, who obviously tried so hard to find a spark of the person her big, broad-shouldered husband had once been. She had carefully placed several framed photographs of their children around the plain room, visible reminders of the past they shared. She'd even hung a framed cross-stitch of a Bible verse above his single bed. Charlotte guessed it might have once meant something to the couple, and surely still did to Greta.

> Thus will I bless thee while I live: I will lift up my hands in thy name. —Psalm 63:4

But the large hands that had once wrestled life back into all kinds of farm machinery around Bedford now sat folded and weak in his lap. The two last fingers on his left hand had long ago been cut off below the knuckles, the result of an unfortunate accident. And the remaining fingers no longer carried a thin line of grease under the fingernails, as Bob's sometimes did—a working man's badge of honor. Today Bud's gnarled, disfigured hands just looked pink, wrinkled, and trembling.

"Bob Stevenson," Greta repeated, as if saying the name might help jar loose a memory. "You remember Bob."

For a moment Bud studied Charlotte's face, as if he might find Bob there, or might momentarily awaken from the darkness that had clouded his mind—the darkness that had cruelly robbed him of the memories he and his wife had shared over so many years.

Greta fingered the pages of her well-worn Bible, keeping a marker at the place in the New Testament where she had paused her reading. Perhaps she should not have hoped, but Charlotte couldn't blame her for trying.

Charlotte paused, standing awkwardly with her hands in the pockets of the volunteer apron she wore here at the convalescent home. Bud stared at the braided rug, leaning down as if looking for something.

"Where's Lady?" he asked suddenly, still searching between his feet. "I need to feed Lady."

"She's okay." His wife answered without hesitation and reached out to pat him on the arm. "We fed her. Lady's fine."

Their beloved cocker spaniel had been dead for twenty years, Greta had explained to Charlotte last week. Soon it was time for Charlotte to slip quietly out of the room once again, leaving them alone with the fractured pieces of their memories, but with their lifelong love no less intact.

"Is there anything else I can get you?" Charlotte asked as she hovered by the door. Greta shook her head with a smile and mouthed the words *thank you*.

Once out in the tiled hallway, though, Charlotte found the visit had taken more out of her than she'd expected. She had to collect herself as she leaned against the wall.

"Is she really taking care of the dog while we're on vacation?" asked Bud, back in the room.

"Yes, dear." Greta's voice took on that soothing teacher's

sound once again, with her charming accent. "You don't have to worry about a thing. Now, do you want me to keep reading?"

She paused a moment, and then took up again where she had apparently left off: "...beareth all things, believeth all things, hopeth all things, endureth all things..."

Charlotte sighed. Though she had heard the familiar words often over the years, and though they had truly comforted her many times, this time they only brought a lump to her throat. She thought of Greta's faithfulness and imagined how she would feel if her own Bob were sitting in the same recliner here at the convalescent center. She couldn't help wondering if God would ever ask so much of her.

It would be too much, God. I could never...

She took another deep breath to try and dismiss such a morbid thought, straightened out her apron, and looked up to see Pastor Nathan Evans striding in her direction, a smile on his face.

"I hoped I'd see you here, Charlotte!" His voice boomed down the long, polished hallway, and she managed several steps before they met in front of the counter of the central nurses' station. "You're here once a week, right?"

"I don't know how you keep track of everyone," she replied. "I'm here one or two days a week. It varies."

"Oh, he knows everybody here, dear." Angelina, the duty nurse seated behind the counter, looked up from her clipboard. "You should know that. He knows your birthday, he knows your dog's name, he probably knows your social security number."

Pastor Evans laughed. "You make me sound pretty sinister."

Angelina had a point, though. Charlotte knew that between here, the hospital, and a scattered parish that included many square miles of town and farms, Pastor Evans could be counted on to visit anyone in need.

"I was here visiting Gladys Visser." Pastor Evans smiled. "You know she fractured her hip in a fall last week."

Charlotte nodded. "I checked in on her earlier today. She's doing a lot better."

As they chatted they walked down the hall of the facility, past the rooms of patients for whom the term *convalescent center* still held the hope of actual convalescence. A blue-haired woman pushing a walker paused to let them pass, but not before Pastor Evans stopped to shake her hand and exchange greetings.

"Actually, Charlotte, it's a good thing I ran into you today. I'm wondering if you've had a chance to speak with Nancy yet?"

"Actually, no." Charlotte paused, trying to remember if Nancy Evans, the pastor's wife, had bumped into her in the checkout line at Herko's or somewhere else. Nothing came to mind. "Not since last Sunday, at least."

"I see. Well, I suppose it wouldn't hurt for me to ask you, then. You see, I don't know if you've heard, but we're planning a young couples' retreat in a few weeks."

"I saw it mentioned in the bulletin." Charlotte wondered how this could possibly relate to her and Bob. "But I have to admit I didn't pay too much attention."

When Pastor Evans laughed, his dark eyes twinkled and his large front teeth flashed. It was easy to see why the man was so popular, with his open, friendly way.

"Of course you didn't. You and Bob just celebrated, what, your forty-sixth anniversary, right?"

Charlotte nodded and once again marveled at what this man remembered about his flock. Even so, she still didn't recognize any connection between an anniversary and the retreat.

"So I was wondering if you—you and Bob—might be willing to speak to the group, perhaps share some of your secrets. You know, after more than forty years, what makes for a good marriage? A few tips, some practical advice, whatever you like. I know the young couples would appreciate hearing from you—especially since I think they can identify more with you than they can with, well, some of the other members of the congregation who aren't as young at heart."

Charlotte chuckled at his delicate reference to age, and then nodded as he went on.

"You know, since your grandkids moved in with you, you can talk to these couples like grandparents, and in a way as young parents too. I'm sure you both have plenty of stories to tell. But it wouldn't be about parenting, necessarily. More about, you know, keeping a marriage strong—the relationship. That kind of thing."

"The relationship. I see." Charlotte hadn't meant to stop short or look so surprised. They waited silently for another resident to wheel by in her chair.

"You don't have to answer me now," Pastor Evans told her when she didn't respond immediately. "Why don't you ask Bob when you get home, and you can tell Nancy or me when you get a chance. But you know we would really appreciate it."

"Of course." Charlotte's head spun as she imagined herself asking Bob to speak in front of a group, no matter how friendly. "How soon do you need to know?"

"Well . . ." He held up his hands in apology. "I don't mean to rush you, but we're printing up a schedule . . . tomorrow. That doesn't matter though. We can adjust. Don't worry about a thing."

"And it's just a small group?"

"Absolutely. We expect maybe nine or ten couples, at the most. You don't have to stay for the entire day, unless you'd like to. We'll start out the morning with your short session, maybe thirty minutes, followed perhaps by a question-and-answer time and refreshments. Very informal. And as I said, I know they would all appreciate hearing a little wisdom from you two."

A little wisdom. She wanted to tell him he should be asking Greta Harbinger rather than her. He should ask someone whose faith and whose marriage vows had probably been tested in ways Charlotte could hardly imagine.

But naturally she couldn't bring herself to mention it. And as she drove home a few minutes later Charlotte pondered what little wisdom she might pass along—*if* Bob agreed to the plan, and that seemed highly unlikely. Surely Pastor Evans would have known that. But since he asked anyway, Charlotte thought it part of her Christian duty to agree, and she prayed that perhaps her husband might see it that way as well—even if speaking to a small group lay well outside his comfort zone.

"I'll do it if you want me to, Lord," she prayed quietly as she approached the farm in the gathering dusk. Actually, she thought she might even enjoy it. "But you know Bob . . ."

She loved her earnest, hardworking husband—despite his faults. It would be out of character for Bob to stand up and speak of what had kept their marriage strong over four decades, three children, and five grandchildren—three of whom had come to live with them on the farm after their daughter died last year.

Bob was a wonderful husband and father. But speak in front of a group, talk about his personal life? Bob just didn't do that sort of thing.

Did he?

As she wondered, she drove through patches of fog that hung low over the land, blanketing fields of tall Nebraska corn now ready for harvesting. It was a few weeks late this year, but it was ready now, and she hoped the rain would hold off until they could get it all in.

The ground fog swirled in dark eddies, making way for her little car with such reluctance that she felt compelled to ease off the gas pedal. Out in the field nearest Heather Creek Road, off to the left, she could barely make out the approaching headlights of their combine. Her son Pete would be at the wheel, making the most of this fall weather. Working overtime once again. The combine's lights flickered in the dusk, and then went out entirely.

Strange, she thought. *I hope he didn't break down again. Not out there in the dark.*

As she worried for her son, a cold drizzle began to wet her windshield.

Chapter Two

The sleet pinged off the windshield of the aging red combine and the patches of ground fog cut down his visibility. Pete paused at the controls and pulled the combine momentarily out of gear, wondering at the strange grinding noise below his seat.

"Not again, you old bucket of rust!" He stomped his left foot, and it sounded against the tender floorboards, which had seen far too many Nebraska winters. Then he listened again to see if he could pinpoint the noise.

Thrum-thrum . . . The unmuffled engine beneath his feet made it hard to hear anything, even the rustling of cornstalks as they were caught between the three fingers of the old corn head—that giant, hand-like picking attachment mounted out ahead of him, which grabbed and shredded three rows of stalks before passing them up a conveyor belt. The side-mounted auger, which spun slowly at the base of the fingers, grabbed stalks and corncobs on their way up to the conveyor belts and a large hopper behind him. That's probably what made most of the squeaking and squealing noises.

But this sound was different. Sort of a jamming and squealing noise. Something wasn't right. But stepping outside into the sleet wasn't too appealing.

Better to keep at it, he thought. *Otherwise we'll never finish this harvest.*

Already it had been delayed by last spring's abnormally wet weather and flooding. Delayed by cooler temperatures at just the wrong stages of the growing cycle. Delayed by equipment breakdowns, which pushed the harvest window later than he liked.

I could have been home on the couch by now, he told himself, *watching another episode of* Ultimate Survivor.

Instead he fiddled with the controls to the cab heater, which seemed to stick all the way on or all the way off. He hiked up the collar of his favorite red and black plaid shirt.

He could have been done by now if they had invested in a newer combine that could run a much wider corn head. A newer cab with climate control and a stereo system and a GPS would have been cool too. They had to keep nursing this old junk.

On the plus side, this combine did feature an old automotive-style AM radio. Pete gave it a good swat once more to try to get the local country station to come in. It stubbornly sputtered and buzzed, and for a moment he could barely make out the sound of country legend Randy Travis singing about loving his sweetheart forever before it dissolved once more into static.

"Shoot!" Pete hit the radio again, harder, but it refused to cooperate. "I like that song."

Fiddling with the radio only made him swerve across a

corn row sideways, so he hunkered down once more and returned to the up-and-back driving through the fields at three miles an hour.

The words of the song had been haunting him, making him think of Dana, especially the part about the promise and how he'd be hers until the day that he died. The thought didn't startle him, anymore, though it seemed no less scary. In fact, on the one-to-ten scale of serious, Pete knew he had crossed over to eleven or twelve, not that he was about to admit that to anyone else. Not yet.

"Keep dreaming, farmer boy," he told himself, swatting at the cab with the back of his hand and rapping his knuckles in the process. "You think she's going to be interested in hooking up with a losing operation like this?"

He was afraid he already knew the answer, and it wasn't good.

"Always just one season away from going under. One season away from losing our shirts. Why would a girl like that want anything to do with a sorry farmer like me?"

He wondered how Dana thought of the future from behind her well-organized desk in her well-organized classroom. From there everything always seemed so predictable, so measurable, like the lesson plans she was always working on and the reports he'd seen her prepare for the parents of her students. Numbers in columns. Big words like *assessment* and *cognitive*. Dana always knew what was going to happen next week and next year. She had it planned out to the minute, in writing.

He didn't know the answers to any of his doubts, except one. Randy Travis's country ballad had raised a question the answer to which was clear.

Would he really love her forever and ever?

He sighed as he started to crank the steering wheel, following the twin beams of his headlights through a pocket of fog.

Just ahead, on Heather Creek Road, he noticed a car's headlights flash by, and then the red flash of brake lights before the little car backed up. Pete hit his own brakes to see why. At the same time, his nephew Sam jumped out of the car and ran toward him, hands waving. Pete throttled down and popped his head out of the cab.

"What's up?" he yelled before Sam reached him, and an unexpected puff of smoke hit him in the face. In the next instant he caught sight of what Sam was waving and yelling about.

"Get out!" hollered Sam. "You're going to blow up!"

Pete wasted no time switching off the ignition, throwing open the door, and jumping to the stubble-laced ground. A quick glance at the rear end of the big machine showed smoke and flames shooting from one of the engine compartments, where gears, pulleys, and dried corn stalks must have ignited. Not serious, but definitely not good.

"I saw the flames as I was driving by." Sam stood by breathlessly and pointed. "Don't you have a fire extinguisher or something?"

There was a fire extinguisher holder bolted to the inside of the driver's-side door, just above their heads, but Pete couldn't remember the last time he'd seen an actual extinguisher mounted there. They could only stand by and watch as the flames gradually died down to a smoldering mess. Pete parked his hands on his hips and waited it out.

"So what happens now?" asked Sam, squinting in the harsh glare of the combine's floodlights.

"I take it apart, I clean it out, I replace the belt or whatever else is fried in there, and I put it back together." Pete didn't mean to sound quite so discouraged, but at the moment it was pretty hard to sound positive.

"I didn't know your combine thing could shoot flames like that."

"It's not the first time."

"So you need some help?"

Pete thought about it for a moment. A little help actually sounded good right about now. Maybe Sam could go get the tools, most of which were in Pete's pickup at the other end of the field. But then again, he could probably fix it just as quickly by himself.

"Thanks anyway, Sam. But you don't want to mess around with a lame combine. Go home and get some dinner." He motioned with his thumb toward the house, hidden behind uncut stalks of corn but still obvious from the faint glow in the distance.

"I'm late already."

"Yeah, but Mom—I mean Grandma—is probably worried that you slid off into a ditch or got hit by lightning or something. Late practice tonight?"

Sam nodded. "Coach Mendenhall is starting to push pretty hard. We were doing wind sprints for an hour, back and forth."

Pete kicked at a clump of weeds between the shaved rows of what was once corn.

"I know about back and forth. But you like it, right? That's your game."

Of course soccer was Sam's game. Why else would he drive all the way to Harding a couple of times a week, and in nasty October weather like this?

"Sure." Sam shrugged. "But you should have seen the field this afternoon. With all the mud, we could really do some good slide tackles."

Pete chuckled. Sure enough, Sam's face and arms were still covered in mud. And in the combine's shadows his grin looked like a Cheshire cat's.

"Yeah, well, you let us know when your games are. Maybe we can come watch, if we can get this combine running and this harvest wrapped up."

"Yeah." Sam didn't quite sound as if he believed it.

"You shouldn't be standing around here looking at broken-down farm equipment. You have homework."

"Don't remind me. Anyway, you're right. I don't need Grandma on my case any more than she already is."

Pete waved his hand and coughed at a wisp of acrid smoke from the back end of the combine. Stupid old machine. Right now he would prefer to shoot it, and put it out of its misery. He should have done that a long time ago.

"I said go. Do your homework, call your girlfriend. This'll just take a few minutes."

Pete knew this breakdown would put him behind even more. Two or three hours, at least, and probably more. In any case, it would be another late night.

"If you're sure—"

"Sure I'm sure."

Pete rubbed his hands together and knelt next to the

problem, just to get an idea what he was up against. *Let's see* ... He would need a couple of toolboxes that he had left in the back of his pickup, a socket set, and ...

He turned to see Sam running back to his idling little sports car, kicking at an imaginary soccer ball as he did. When Sam pulled open his door a blast of pounding rock music filled the evening. No Randy Travis there.

Pete watched as Sam tossed the ball in the air and tapped it expertly into his car with his foot before climbing in and driving off toward the distant glow of the house.

Chapter Three

"Give it here, Christopher." Sam reached to retrieve his soccer ball. "I need it for practice after school."

"Christopher." Charlotte warned them from where she was standing at the sink. "Don't tease him, please. You know what can happen."

Just then Sam's little brother knocked over his orange juice and spilled it all over the kitchen table. It started to drip on Emily's lap. With a yelp she held up the book she was reading as she backed her chair away from the table.

"Christopher!" She glared at her little brother. "Do you always have to be spilling something or making a mess?"

"Not always," mumbled Christopher, dabbing at the mess with his paper napkin. "Just sometimes."

His napkin did little to hold back the tide of juice that had now spread across the table, so Charlotte fetched a dishrag from the sink.

"You kids need to get to school now," she told them. "Just get this cleaned up first. And Sam, did you say you've got soccer practice in Harding this afternoon?"

"Yup," he answered. "Same as usual."

Emily was the first to leave the table, but the boys managed to mop up the worst of the mess.

"Smooth move." Sam elbowed Christopher as they left to gather their things. "If you weren't squirreling around, none of this would have happened."

"If you weren't so bossy," countered Christopher, "it wouldn't have happened either."

"Boys!" Charlotte warned them again. "Don't—"

Christopher lunged for the ball one last time, but Sam pivoted and evaded him.

"And he fakes out one more defender . . ." said Sam, dribbling the ball with his feet as he ran out the door.

"COME ON, FARMER BOY." The defender in the white jersey grunted as he lunged for the soccer ball. "Give it your best shot."

The boy's bushy dark hair flew out like a banner in the crisp afternoon air as he worked to keep Sam from approaching the goal. This guy so obviously telegraphed which way he was going to move before he moved, it was easy for a good ball handler like Sam to fake him out and dribble right by.

"Sorry, Mike." Sam grinned as he played around. They might be on the same team, and this might just be a scrimmage during the regular afternoon practice, but Sam wasn't holding back this time the way he usually had before. Today he would show Coach Mendenhall what he could do.

By this time two more defenders had come to Mike's rescue, but Sam knew he could do the same thing to them that he had to Mike. In a move he had practiced over and over at home, he first faked left, then tapped the top of the ball to stop it completely, then whirled to his right and slipped around one hapless defender. The other kid had no idea which way to turn or how to react. That left Sam free to tap the ball between the next guy's legs, which made the defender look even more foolish than he already did.

"Hey, what?" mumbled the other boy. But Sam wasn't sticking around for a conversation with any of the Harding boys. They had no clue what Sam could do, and for now, that was just the way Sam liked it.

He rejoined his ball behind the defender, ignoring his teammate Josh across the field, who waved to get his attention. Josh may have had an open shot right now, but Sam was taking this one in himself.

Ten steps brought him nearly in front of the goal, where the goalkeeper, crouched and tensed in anticipation, swayed from side to side. One last defender stood between them.

"Sam!" yelled Josh, waving his hand from just ten yards away. "Over here!"

Passing the ball would have been the play from Coach Mendenhall's official playbook. Pass across the field for Josh to score. The problem was Josh had a habit of missing even the easiest goal-on shots. Sam had been keeping track of the right wing for the past several practices and hadn't been overly impressed. He seemed like a nice guy, but with two left feet.

Not this time, Josh.

Sam wound up and swung his left foot as if he were going to continue the play by sending it across to Josh. But without warning he pulled back instead with his right, jamming the ball into the corner of the net, past the last defender and behind the keeper's back. *Goal!* The keeper didn't even see it flash by.

"Yes!" Sam pumped his fist in the air as he trotted by the keeper and circled back onto the field.

"Nice shot." Josh held up a wimpy high five but didn't smile. "But I was wide open."

Open, my man, thought Sam, *but not ready.*

None of the other kids wearing the bright blue jerseys of the Harding Recreation League Pioneers had been ready either. Not one of them was half as good as his old teammates back in San Diego. In fact, he would have liked to see his old team visit Nebraska to teach these guys a lesson or two in ball handling. He brushed against Mike on his way back to the sidelines to get a drink of water. Not a bad way to wrap up another practice.

"Good thing I'm not a farmer boy, huh?" Sam did his best to hold back a grin as he trotted by. Mike just frowned at him the way he always did. Coach Mendenhall motioned for Sam to join him on the sidelines, most likely for a nice pat on the back.

But as Sam approached, he noticed Coach was not smiling. He kept his arms folded on his chest, offering no clue about what he would say. Sam tried to look like he wasn't out of breath as he trotted up to the bench.

"You know how to handle that ball," began the coach. This sounded like high praise indeed.

"Thanks." Sam relaxed a little at the compliment. "Back in San Diego, we used to—"

"This isn't San Diego, Sam." The coach cut him off, his eyes still on the rutted field. "And you'd be a lot better off if you remembered that."

"Sorry... what?" All of a sudden Sam wasn't following, and he fought off a sinking feeling in the pit of his stomach.

"Now, you look out there and you tell me how many guys you count on a team."

Sam didn't have to look, except away from the coach's face. Where was this going?

"Eleven," he whispered.

"What's that?" Coach Mendenhall raised his voice. "I didn't hear you."

"I said eleven." When Sam raised his voice several of the other guys stared in his direction to see what was going on. This time there was nowhere to hide.

"Eleven, huh?" Coach began to pace, the way he did when they had to run sprints and no one was running quickly enough to suit him. "Well, that's just amazing. 'Cause from what I just saw out there, I could have sworn I saw a one-man team. I saw a guy who had no use for the other ten. Ever heard of such a thing? Or maybe you just forgot the play."

Now it was Sam's turn to turn a little red in the face. How was he supposed to answer that? But Coach was waiting for Sam to say something.

"I didn't forget." Sam finally tried to explain, and he found his voice cracking this time. "I just thought I had a better shot."

"You thought you had a better shot." Coach repeated the line once more for emphasis. "Well, Mr. Slater. Maybe where you come from, your coach was okay with that kind of playing. So let's give you the benefit of the doubt."

Sam swallowed hard as the coach went on.

"But I'll tell you what. Around here we don't go for that kind of hotdogging. I don't care how many goals you think you can score, or how well you can dribble the ball through the legs of your defenders. If that's the way you want to play, you're going to be sitting out the rest of the season. There's more to this game than just talent, and you're going to have to show you know how to play like a member of the team. Got it?"

Sam nodded and started to turn away, but the coach caught his jersey.

"One more thing, Sam." Now his voice had begun to settle down and he released his grip. "Don't get me wrong. I like how hard you've been working. I wish half the other guys on the team worked as hard as you. You guys hear that?"

Several of Sam's teammates looked up from where they were getting drinks of water, as if startled. Now he was talking to the entire group of eighteen young men, the entire club. Some held soccer balls under their arms and others sipped water from paper cups. But they all came to attention at the sound of their coach's reprimand.

"So listen to me, you guys. We'll never win game one if we don't start playing like a team, got it? You know the plays. We've been over the fundamentals. I want to see more passing, less hotdogging. And that goes for all of you!" He paused and shook his head. "All right. Now, take a lap and get out of here. I'll see you again."

He pointed at one of the quickly retreating jerseys. "And Slater, don't be late next time!"

That went well, Sam thought as he retreated. *I'm making all kinds of friends here.*

He plodded around the perimeter of the field alone, keeping his distance from the packs of three or four guys who made their way around the field before grabbing their stuff to leave. No one seemed to want to talk anyway; the guys even ignored a cluster of Harding High cheerleaders who had been watching football practice.

A street lamp at the far end of the distant parking lot flickered as it brightened, adding to the spilled light from the football stadium. The air smelled like frost and burning leaves.

Just ahead of Sam, several of his teammates walked in the same direction, but at a careful distance. Josh lugged a too-large duffel bag over his slight shoulders. Honestly, the kid looked almost as funny off the field as he looked on it. Josh looked back at Sam but didn't slow down.

"Hey, farmer boy!" He heard Mike's voice coming from behind him. Sam didn't turn around, but Mike caught up just the same. "You sure got Coach fired up."

"Wasn't trying to."

"Fine. But if you're warming the bench during a game, then that college scout from U of N won't notice you."

"Wait a minute. What?" Sam wasn't sure if Mike was serious or what. "Who said anything about a college scout?"

Mike smiled and looked around now that he had attracted a better audience.

"Farmer boy here hasn't heard about the college scout. Should I tell him?" The other players didn't answer, so he went on with his story. "A college scout. You know what a college scout is."

Of course he did. Mike held his hands up in mock surrender.

"All I'm saying is what one of the football coaches told me. He's my math teacher, you know? And he said that the U of N is sending a couple of scouts to our games."

"When?"

"I don't know. They're not saying when. All they said is it would be a football guy, and they thought a soccer guy too. Just thought you'd want to know."

This was awesome—if it were really true.

"Or maybe," added Mike, "you'll be too busy milking cows to come next time."

Sam might have snapped back once more. But this time he only felt tired, and he let it go.

"Don't forget." Mike lowered his voice into a silly imitation of Coach Mendenhall. "More passing, less hotdogging."

Sam smirked. By that time they had reached the nearly empty parking lot, where several of the boys had parked their cars and pickup trucks. He'd parked his low-slung little Datsun sports car in the only spot available at the time, at the far corner of the lot. And though he could hardly see in the late afternoon dusk, he could see enough to notice his car had tilted to the side just a bit. A stray beam of stadium light was just bright enough to show him what had happened, and he groaned.

"Perfect," he mumbled as he fumbled with his keys. He pulled open the back end, hoping his spare tire hadn't gone flat as well.

Chapter Four

Charlotte looked out through the window once more to check for approaching headlights, and tried to tell herself not to worry that Sam was an hour late coming home.

"He'll be here in just a moment," she said, keeping her eyes glued on the road, Lightning cradled in her arms. She felt herself cycling between irritation and downright worry. Sam wasn't always on time for everything, but he wasn't ever this late either. And at night, on slick roads, in his little car . . . she tried unsuccessfully not to think of what could happen. She called his cell phone again, but it went straight to voice mail.

At least Christopher and Emily were both safely upstairs, presumably working on homework but probably texting their friends or playing video games. Pete and Bob were out repairing the combine again, and had pulled it up next to the barn so they could better see what they were doing. Pete had been giving his father a hard time for being an old man and needing a lot of light to see what was going on. Charlotte knew that if that old machine made it through one more harvest, she'd be shocked. On the other hand, she prayed her husband would make it through many more.

She tried not to think about how she would ask Bob about the couples' seminar, or when. He was just too busy this time of year. His mind was always occupied with talk of combines and harvesting schedules.

Either that, she thought, *or I'm just too chicken to ask. I know what he's going to say.*

A pair of headlights flashed by out on the road and for a moment she thought maybe it was Sam, but the lights turned away and the car continued down the road. She had already washed and put away all the dinner dishes, except for the plate of meat loaf, green beans, and mashed potatoes she'd covered with plastic wrap and left in the microwave to reheat.

"I thought he'd be here by now," she told Lightning, scratching her ear and hearing a low purr. She rocked the cat like a baby and let pictures of quilt patterns flash through her mind to pass the time. Then she tried to think of them in color but finally gave up and let the purring of the cat soothe her while she shifted to Bible verses that would remind her not to worry. But they escaped her as well.

Finally another pair of distant headlights caught her eye, and she sighed with relief when they slowed and pulled into the driveway.

She put the cat down and hurried for the kitchen to start the microwave. "I'm telling you, Lightning, he'd better have a very good excuse."

Toby, her faithful dog, who had been sleeping by

Charlotte's feet, suddenly awoke from her dreams, lifted her nose in the air, and trotted between the front room and the back door. A minute later Sam pushed open the back door and stepped inside, letting in a rush of cold air and a tumble of dried leaves with him.

His cheeks looked chapped and red from the cold, and his sweats were muddy. Nothing new there. Charlotte had long ago resigned herself to the inevitable fact that boys and mud went together. She uncrossed her arms with some effort, softened her expression, and clutched the steaming dinner plate with a couple of her harvest-themed pot holders.

"I saved you some dinner," she told him. "Why don't you clean up and come sit down?"

"Oh, I . . ." He paused in mid-stride, still holding his worn backpack. "I didn't think you'd do that."

"What do you mean? We eat dinner here every evening, same time, same place." She tried hard to keep the edge off her voice, and she determined she would wait for him to volunteer his excuse for being so late.

"Yeah, I know, Grandma. But my tire was flat again when I got done with practice. Took me a few minutes to change it."

"I hope your spare was good this time?" She raised her eyebrows in question. As concerned as she was, this wasn't the first time, and this flat-tire situation was something akin to the I-ran-out-of-gas excuse.

"Yeah, but then, turns out I was getting hungry, so I stopped for a burger on the way home. So I'm not really that . . ."

His voice trailed off when he noticed the way her face fell. Then he obviously scrambled to correct what he had been about to tell her.

"I'm not really that full. You know, it was just a snack. Smells good. Your food always smells good."

"Now you're just trying to work your way out of a jam with flattery." She set his plate down and peeled away the plastic wrap. Hungry or not, she wasn't about to let Sam waste food.

She watched as he washed his hands in the sink, and then returned to his plate and dug in without bowing his head. Did they not offer enough of an example, giving thanks at every meal they ate together? Although, when she thought about it, she couldn't quite remember the last meal they'd all eaten together.

Sam dug in. If he was full from the hamburger, he showed no sign of it. She remembered how Pete could put away the food just as well in his day. In fact, he could still put away the food.

"So how was practice?" She ventured an innocent question to get him talking as she poured him a glass of milk. Sam only stuffed another bite of meat loaf in his mouth before looking up and making a noise.

She chased a puddle on the counter next to the sink with a sponge and straightened the forks in her silverware drawer. But when she turned a moment later, Sam had launched into the mashed potatoes. It would take another couple of minutes before he mopped the remaining tomato sauce from the plate with a piece of bread, polished off his second glass of milk, and pushed his chair back with a screech.

"You never told me about practice," she said. He looked up at her with surprise, as if hearing her question for the first time.

"Oh, practice? The same, I guess."

"You like Coach Mendenhall?"

"He's okay." Sam snagged the strap of his backpack and made for the living room.

"How about the other boys? Are you making any friends?"

He paused at the archway between the kitchen and the living room, his back toward her, and shrugged the same way Christopher often did. "They all go to Harding High. I'm the only one from Bedford."

"Is that a no? Are they nice?"

"They're okay."

"So the coach is okay and the kids are okay, but you're not getting to know anybody, is that right? I thought you really wanted to play on this team."

Charlotte felt like an interrogator, but she didn't know how else to draw Sam out. Yet when he audibly sighed and his shoulders slumped she feared she had crossed the line. Finally Sam turned to face her, and no, he didn't look happy.

"I did really want to play, Grandma. It's the only team around that I can be on. But Coach Mendenhall is really hard-nosed, and none of the other guys are any good. Not like we were in San Diego. I have a feeling we're going to lose every game we play."

"Oh, honey, how do you know? Don't you think you'd better give it a chance?"

"I am giving it a chance. But I know, Grandma. I've been on teams before, and this is the worst one I've ever been on."

"But you can't keep comparing what's here to what you remember from California. It's just different now."

"You got that right."

"You're not going to quit, are you?"

Sam didn't answer, just frowned and turned away. This time Charlotte let him go, even if he had left his dirty plate and glass on the table and his chair not pushed in, and even if he hadn't thanked her for warming up his plate.

She prayed quietly for him as his heavy footsteps thumped up the stairs.

Please don't let him quit, Lord. Help him to not compare everything to the way it used to be. Help him to get to know some of the boys better.

She grabbed Sam's plate to rinse it in the sink just as Pete came stomping in the back door—act two in this evening's frustrated and filthy boys drama. He stood outlined in the door for a moment as if trying to decide whether to come in.

"We could leave the door open like that and warm up the yard for you," she told him. "Or you could take off your boots and come in."

"Thanks." He kicked off his muddy boots on the mat with all the other muddy boots and unrecognizable sneakers and finally stepped inside. Hadn't she just been thinking about boys and dirty socks?

"So I'm afraid to ask if you got it fixed." She reached for the refrigerator. "Glass of milk?"

"No, no thanks." He shook his head and stood in the middle of the kitchen in his greasy, dusty overalls. "I just want to know something. Didn't you guys ever have a conversation about replacing some of that old harvesting equipment? Because I tell you, I have just had it with fixing that old stuff over and over and over again. Dad says it's fine, that I just need to maintain it better. But when something is held together with baling wire and bubble gum, what's there to maintain? Doesn't he think that our time is worth something too?"

"I take it you've been discussing this with your father lately?"

She knew it wouldn't be right to gang up on Bob, who couldn't defend himself at the moment. Better just to listen.

"Are you kidding? I've shown him what the new equipment can do. How much time we can save. He just doesn't get it."

"Oh, I think he does. You two just see things differently."

"You think so? Well, I'm not sure he's seeing much of anything these days. Even with his reading glasses he's blind as a bat."

"You're exaggerating."

"No, I'm not. I saw him trying to read a shop manual the other day. He was holding it out at arm's length, squinting and rubbing his eyes and all kinds of stuff. And he still couldn't read it. He's blind. Even the kids are noticing it."

"Wait until you get to be his age."

"I know, Mom. But another thing. Give me one good reason we should still be working with a three-row corn head. Only three rows at a time! Between using this antique equipment and all the time we spend welding and patching and making do, I could probably harvest this field a lot faster with a horse team."

Charlotte had to laugh at the thought of Pete out in the field behind a couple of horses.

"You're laughing, Mom. But I'm serious. It's like we're still living in the last century. It's pitiful."

"You forget what year this is. Most everything we own is actually still from the last century."

"You know what I mean. From the eighteen hundreds."

"Now you're exaggerating."

"Not much. Have you seen the equipment I'm talking about? It's got welds on welds on . . . oh, forget it."

He stood in the middle of the kitchen, his hands clasped behind his head as if in pain. Venting. Perhaps it was good for him, and good for Charlotte to just listen. She pointed toward the refrigerator once more.

"You sure you don't want a glass of milk?"

"No. I mean, yeah, I'm sure. I've got some back at my apartment."

"From this century?"

Pete didn't laugh as he turned back to the door and slipped his muddy boots back on. But the mother instinct in Charlotte told her Pete hadn't come into the kitchen just to complain about old farm equipment.

"Pete," she said, "is there something else you needed?"

She had probably asked him too late. He stood with his back to her and a hand on the doorknob, and for a moment he didn't answer. Then he looked back over his shoulder at her.

"No, I was just . . . I don't know. All this stuff about the combine, it just makes me wonder how we're going to keep going next year, and the year after that. You ever wonder that? I mean, like when Dad asked you to marry him, did you look at this operation and think, 'Wow, there's the future of farming?'"

When Dad asked you to marry him? Now *there* was an interesting way of framing the question.

Charlotte thought for a moment before answering. "That was a long time ago, Pete. I don't know. Your father was very charming. Strong. A hard worker. I suppose it never crossed my mind, the way you put it."

"Not even a little bit?"

"Pete! You make it sound like his proposal was some kind of business investment. We were starting a family. I had plenty of other things to worry about. And as far as the farm was concerned, I have always trusted your father to do the right thing. You should too."

"I didn't mean it that way." He took a deep breath. "I was just thinking that if I was going to . . ." His voice trailed off, and she waited for him to finish his thought, but he must have changed his mind.

"Forget it. But listen, don't tell Dad I was, you know, complaining. He's already heard it all, and I don't think he's changing his mind for now."

"Maybe not, Pete. But you know he always respects your opinions."

"Right." He yanked open the door and headed back out into the dark, back to his little apartment over the tractor shed. And again her mother's instinct made her wonder.

Chapter Five

It was Saturday afternoon, and Christopher didn't care that it was only forty-two degrees out in the North Quarter of the Stevenson farm, with relative humidity at 52 percent, scattered clouds and a wind chill factor that brought down the temperature several degrees. He wiped his drippy nose on the arm of his ripped-at-the-elbows play jacket, checked his homemade weather station once more, and recited the weather report out loud, in case anyone in the listening audience wanted to know.

"Overall, folks, looks like a chilly but gorgeous autumn day," he said in the deepest weatherman voice he owned. He thought that made him sound more like a pro, rather than just a sixth grader.

He crossed his arms and looked around at his secret spot, directly underneath the rusty legs of the long-abandoned windmill that was tucked away on the top of a rise in the North Quarter and out of sight of the main house. He'd chosen this spot because no one could see him here, unless they had a reason to come looking. That made it a good hideaway. Not even Toby knew he was out here every day after school.

The best part was the windmill. Grandpa told him they had stopped using it a long time ago, but it was still extremely cool. A heavy steel shaft hung down like the pendulum of a grandfather clock, just above his head, and it probably would have hit an adult on the head. Up on the windmill part, half the blades were missing, but the rest of them still tried to turn whenever the wind picked up. That's when it started squeaking and groaning, and the old tower shook as if it might fall down.

But that doesn't scare me, he told himself. *I could get out of the way anytime I wanted to.*

It wouldn't fall down now, not with winds out of the north at just four miles per hour, the way his homemade anemometer told him. He adjusted the paper Dixie cup of his carefully constructed instrument as it spun around and around on four plastic straws. He just had to count how many times it spun around in sixty seconds, using the second hand of his watch, and then he would double that to know how fast the wind was blowing in feet per minute.

"Thirteen, fourteen, fifteen . . ." How was that for advanced math?

His teacher, Ms. Luka, had been pretty impressed when he'd told her what he was doing for his project, and how the anemometer worked. And the anemometer had been easier to make than it was for most people to pronounce the word, except that he'd been practicing. Weather guys would know how to say the word. Anemometer. Wind meter. Same difference.

He squinted up again at the slowly turning blades of the bigger windmill, which looked lopsided and terribly noisy, and he could still make out the faded lettering on the tail: "The Aermotor Co., Chicago."

What kind of a word was *Aermotor*, he wondered? Probably when people had made that thing, way back when, maybe they didn't know how to spell very good, or very well.

He turned to the wagon loaded with a five-gallon red plastic jug he'd found in the barn. He was pretty sure it was once used for gas—that's what it had smelled like. But a couple of rinses fixed that. And a slow drip from the wagon told him why Grandpa didn't need it for keeping fuel anymore. If he hurried, it was still okay for hauling water to his secret project. He knelt down next to one of the windmill's legs and reached into the little garden plot he'd created among the four steel legs.

"How are we doing today, Mr. Pumpkin? Putting on a few pounds? That's good. You can get as fat as you like. In fact, the fatter the better."

He stroked the smooth skin of the largest pumpkin he'd ever seen outside of a grocery store—easily bigger than a beach ball, and lopsided in sort of a weird-looking, blobby way. It reminded him of a cartoon, like a radioactive mud creature let loose in a city, where people would scream and run away as it blobbed all over the place. But like the silly cartoon creature, this real-life pumpkin was growing larger every day, for sure.

He undid the top of the water jug and let it dribble down in just the right place, just as he'd done many times before. Too bad the windmill didn't work the way it was supposed to, so the wind could automatically pump water and he wouldn't have to come here all the time to water his secret pumpkin patch.

"But I don't mind," he told the pumpkin. "You're going to keep growing and we're going to win the official *Bedford Leader* Annual Giant Pumpkin Contest, right?"

As he bent down near the pumpkin, a fresh set of tire tracks, big and wide and deep, caught his eye. He was no crime-scene investigator, but these were nothing like tractor tracks, which Christopher might have expected here. And nothing like the regular old tire tracks from Lazarus, Uncle Pete's old pickup. He looked at them first from one angle and then another. The double tracks seemed to stop right up here next to the old windmill, then back out. No doubt about it.

Somebody's been up here, Christopher thought, checking out the other pumpkins. *Maybe a spy, or maybe a burglar.*

Just as he was imagining this scenario, he jumped at the sound of a squeaky wheelbarrow coming his way.

"There you are." Grandpa gave him a little smile as he pulled up to the top of the rise, next to where Christopher was kneeling at the base of the windmill. "Wasn't sure if you'd be here."

"I'm here. Just checking on the prize winner."

"You've sure been keeping it a secret. People are going to find out in a few weeks, you know."

"I know, but that's in a few weeks."

"I get it." He looked a little more closely. "What happened to the other two?"

Christopher shook his head slowly, as if reporting a death. "When I checked on them the other day, something had nibbled the vine. Like they cut it or something with their teeth. But the pumpkins weren't very big anyway."

"Hmm. Well, let's hope that doesn't happen to our number one. He's still doing pretty good?"

"I figure he's gained another ten pounds."

"You think? Hard telling. I'm sure not going to try to lift him—not without some help. But wait till we get another load of secret fertilizer on him. Pretty soon he's going to be too big to fit in the back of the pickup."

Christopher wasn't so sure about that, but he wrinkled his nose as Grandpa found a stick and mixed gray powder in a bucket with water. Then he carefully poured it around the base of the pumpkin plant and stood back to admire their project. As always, it smelled like aged chicken manure.

"Speaking of pickups," Christopher said, "you didn't drive up here in the pickup, did you?"

"Nah." Grandpa bent down a little closer to the big pumpkin. "I don't have any cause to drive up here. Not while my legs are still working."

"And this doesn't look like it came from your tractor, does it?" Christopher stepped over to the tire tracks and pointed.

At first Grandpa didn't seem too concerned, just glanced down at the pattern of the twin ruts. But then he did stop and squint for a moment too.

"*Hmm.* Well, I wouldn't worry about it. Probably some friends of your Uncle Pete's."

"Why would they come up here?"

"No idea. Maybe I'll ask him, if I get a chance."

They both admired the giant pumpkin again.

Grandpa patted the dirt from his knees and nodded his head. "I think it might win though."

"You do?"

"I haven't seen what everybody else is growing, but it has a chance, sure."

Grandpa tossed the bucket back into his dented old green wheelbarrow and held his rough hand out to shake.

"And if it does, partner, you remember our deal."

"I remember." Christopher's hand got lost inside Grandpa's grip, but he shook it with all the seriousness a sixth grader could muster. A deal was a deal, and he would stick to it—as long as his pumpkin survived all the way to the weigh-in. Even though that was only a few weeks away, he was still worried. Especially after all the other pumpkins in his secret patch had withered away.

Christopher looked down at the mysterious tire tracks once again, his head swirling with ideas for security spy cams and burglar alarms.

That's what I need, he decided. *A burglar alarm. Because one way or another I'm going to find out who was messing around up here . . . and why.*

Chapter Six

Late Tuesday afternoon Emily shivered in the cold of the unfinished attic, wishing she had worn a sweater, and wishing even more for a better light than the fading flashlight she'd found.

"There it is." A string dangling from a lone light bulb above her head brushed her cheek, so she grabbed it and pulled—hard. But a moment later she still stood in the dark, the broken string in her hand. This was not the way it was supposed to work.

"Stupid thing." She dropped the string in disgust, and looked for some other way to get around.

The two dormer windows up here in the attic didn't help—it was so dark outside. And of course with her luck the faded beam from the flashlight she'd brought up flickered unless she slapped it with her palm over and over.

Why can't we have a normal light up here? She swept the beam around, about ready to give up her search. Looking up, she could see the bottom side of the roof. Eaves intersected every which way so she could hardly walk through here without bumping her head on some gnarly wooden beam, and who knew what kinds of rusty nails were poking out everywhere? She stepped lightly on old boards that creaked and groaned under her weight.

Still, she remembered her mission, so she crouched lower and kept going, pointing her wimpy, flickering flashlight into the corners and under the eaves. She wondered what kind of creatures might be watching, and fully expected to see a pair of red eyes blinking back at her from the darkness. Instead her light barely made out several dog-eared boxes in the corner. Someone had marked OLD KEEPSAKES on the side of one, CHRISTMAS DECORATIONS on a second, and PHOTO ALBUMS on another.

Naturally the one she wanted would be at the bottom of the pile. She set her flashlight aside for a moment to get at it. The whole thing made her want to sneeze all over again. The boxes felt dusty and nasty, but after a bit of pushing and shuffling she finally managed to pull the photo box free and peer inside.

Sure enough, the box contained a number of old photo albums, some marked with dates and others decorated with scripty gold writing that was pretty much faded and hard to read. The one she was looking for was white with silver trim, with OUR WEDDING on the front.

"Hey! What are you doing up here?" asked Christopher, using his best scary voice. She looked back toward the trap door to see his head poking through.

"Nothing," she told him. "I'm coming right back down. You stay there."

Album in hand, she hurried for the door to keep Christopher from climbing up. He'd been exploring up here before, but that was during the daytime. Right now she didn't need him poking around and getting into trouble.

"Hey," he told her. "I just wanted to see."

"You saw. Now move, so I can get down."

Emily took a deep breath after she had finally clambered back down the pull-down stairway, and shook the dust from her jeans and hair. She had left her flashlight up there, probably still on, and had left the box unpacked, its contents strewn all over the attic floor. Right now she could think of a lot of other things she cared more about.

"I still wanted to check it out," said Christopher, who stood back as she pushed the spring-loaded stairway into place and secured the door. "Remember all those funny costumes we found? It's cool up there."

"Some other time," she told her brother.

"Come on, Emily."

Emily rolled her eyes and made her way downstairs to the kitchen table, where she could examine her find a little more closely. She had decided a long time ago there was no use trying to understand boys, especially not little brothers. Everything she thought was highly gross, he thought was highly cool. There was no sense in it.

Meanwhile, Grandma turned from the kitchen sink where she had her hands buried in soapsuds. It seemed as if Grandma always had her hands buried in soapsuds at the kitchen sink.

"Did you find what you were looking for?" Grandma asked, picking up a towel. Emily plopped the album down on the table and opened to the first page.

"It was kind of buried in a bunch of other old photo albums, but yeah."

Grandma smiled. "I avoid going up there if I can help it. But I see you found the right one."

Emily looked at a photo of a group of people standing in front of a church that she sort of recognized, but sort of didn't.

"Yes, that's the church." Grandma pointed at the steeple. "It looks different because we rebuilt the steeple after it blew down in a storm. But that was years ago."

Emily nodded as Grandma went on.

"I don't know if this will help you with your school project, but we actually did have some very nice photographs taken at our wedding. I think it was your grandfather's best man—an old school buddy—whose cousin was a photographer of some sort for *Look* magazine, or perhaps it was *Life* magazine. Or maybe he just wanted to be. Oh, now I can't remember. In any case, this fellow was a very fine photographer with a lot of fancy equipment, and he was in the area visiting relatives, so—"

"What's *Life* magazine?" Grandma seemed to think it was funny that Emily had never heard of it.

"Oh, I'm sorry. I suppose that was before your time, wasn't it? It was a picture magazine, you know, before the Internet. If you can imagine, it had very nice photographs from things happening all over the world. I'll have to show you a copy of the magazine sometime. I think Grandpa still has several of them saved in a box somewhere. He used to go out and buy a copy when something special happened, like the moon landing."

"You don't think he keeps them up in the attic, do you?"

"Even if he does," Grandma laughed once more, "I won't make you go up there again."

Emily turned back to the people in the black-and-white

photos on page after page of the old album. Most of the people looked rather grim and boring, but Grandma pointed out Grandpa in a black suit and tie, which looked funny.

"I can't believe it," said Emily. "He really had dark hair."

"And lots of it," agreed Grandma.

They both laughed. Grandma obviously liked telling her stories. And she was kind of cute when she tried to sound like a kid.

Emily turned the page and found a photo of Grandma in a pretty white wedding dress with lace and sequins. She had to catch her breath.

"That's you?"

Grandma nodded, a faraway look in her eyes.

"Hard to believe, isn't it? That skinny little thing?"

"Oh, you're still . . . skinny, Grandma."

That made Grandma laugh all over again.

"Now there's a pretty fib." She carefully slipped the photo out of the four corner mounts, one at a time. "But here, why don't you take this one for your fashion report?"

"Actually, it's for a PowerPoint presentation."

"Oh. I have no idea what that is. Power what?"

"PowerPoint. You know. Like a slide show, with pictures and words and stuff."

"I should have guessed. You kids don't use paper anymore, do you?"

"Sure we do. But this report's on the computer. It's for our public speaking class. Ashley and I are working together on ours, except she's doing hers on Princess Diana."

Grandma held out the picture. And when Emily looked

more closely, there was something strangely familiar about the face staring back at her. She couldn't quite put her finger on it though.

"So you can still use the photograph, can't you?" asked Grandma. "Here."

"It's so old." Emily gingerly accepted the photo, holding it by the edges so she wouldn't ruin or smudge it.

"I suppose it is," Grandma agreed. "So you'll want to be very careful with it. Please. It's the only copy I have. Precious memories."

Emily found three other photos showing the gown from different angles as well. She knew enough about wedding gowns to recognize the brilliant white silk, the Empire-line bodice, and the Cornelli embroidery ribbon work. Her grandmother's lace veil extended halfway down her back, and a lovely chapel train swept back from her waist some three or four feet. Oh, and white gloves too! Emily had to admit, Grandma looked very pretty.

"Now here's something else you might want to mention in your fashion power show," added Grandma, flipping through more of the album's pages. "I mean, your report. Anyway, did you know that Great-Aunt Rosemary made my gown?"

"What do you mean, she made it? You mean you didn't buy it from a store?"

"Heavens, no. We couldn't afford such a thing in those days."

"So how did that work?"

"She saw several pictures of society wedding gowns at the time, took a few measurements, and the next thing you know, voila! Of course, she was still making alterations and pinning things up on the morning of the wedding. It made me quite a bit more nervous than I already was. But no one knew any of that except me and her. She was my maid of honor, after all."

"Wow." Emily couldn't believe someone had made it all by hand, especially not when she looked more closely at the gown and saw all the detail. "Did she use one of those sewing machines that was run with the foot pedal, like back and forth, with a pulley? I've seen those in a museum."

"Emily! I'm old, but I'm not that old. We did have electric sewing machines when I was young, you know."

"Oh yeah. And indoor plumbing too, right?"

"I'm going to let Grandpa tell you the outhouse stories, if you want to hear them."

"Not really, Grandma." Emily wrinkled her nose at the thought. "He can tell Sam and Christopher if he wants."

"Good girl. But the sewing—you know that's how we did it in those days. I mean, that's how she did it. I don't think I could have sewn anything this complicated myself. You know how talented Rosemary is."

Emily pulled out a notepad and scribbled a few notes for her report, especially the part about her great-aunt making the dress herself, and how long it took. That would be a cool bit of information.

"I'll scan the photos, Grandma." Already she could imagine how she might place a close-up of the gown on the right side of the slide, with smaller close-ups of details—the lace trim, the veil—fading in and out, one at a time. She could add a few pictures of store-bought gowns from that era, like ads from Sears or something, and then show how the styles had changed. A little old-time piano music in the background would add a fun element.

This PowerPoint report would be the best ever, she decided. Maybe climbing up into that horrible, dark, dusty attic had been worth it after all.

Chapter Seven

Early the next morning Heather Creek seemed wide awake, gurgling contentedly through the little shaded gully where so much had started for Charlotte almost fifty years ago. What better place to retreat to and pray than here at the Engagement Spot?

Carrying a small pocket Bible with her, she found her favorite spot on a cottonwood log Bob had felled and trimmed into a rough bench, like a front-row seat in a wooded amphitheater. She settled easily onto the log and drew the collar of her purple sweater a little more tightly around her neck, waiting patiently for the show to begin.

As if on cue, a little towhee was the first to announce the golden sunrise in the east, whistling a song that always sounded to Charlotte like a cheery "drink your TEA!" She listened carefully, though she could not see the singer. Within a few notes, the bird's friends and family joined in the chorus, while a distant raven punctuated with a percussion of his own calls.

Charlotte closed her eyes and breathed deeply of the pungent cottonwoods, and the earthy damp of decomposing leaves. She listened to the sound of the willing little stream that wound south to the Little Blue River and over the Kansas border to the Kansas River.

A mourning dove announced her own wake-up call, Charlotte's favorite, though she wondered if the doves should not already have been making their way south to Texas for the winter. Perhaps the last couple of mild weeks had swayed them to delay their flight, and for now that seemed good.

Even so, as the golden leaves of the cottonwoods broke free in the gentle morning breeze and fluttered down on her like an early snow, Charlotte knew the more unforgiving cold could not be long delayed. She cracked open her little Bible to the tiny red ribbon marker, which reminded her of where she had left off in the psalm she had memorized as a child.

"The heavens declare the glory of God," she read out loud, looking up as she whispered the words. "The skies proclaim the work of his hands." And here in her tree-canopied hideaway, little patches of the bright blue heavens tinged with streaks of gold opened up like flowers in the sky as the cottonwoods quivered in anticipation of a bright autumn morning. The sight made it easy for her to close her eyes in prayer, and she lifted up her thanks as well as her requests as she thought of Bob and the kids. She prayed quietly as each one came to mind.

She prayed for Sam, who seemed a little more lost than usual, looking for his place on the farm . . . or off it. She wished she could understand better the challenge of a young man facing his future.

Or even a relatively older young man (if there were such

a thing) such as Pete, who seemed no closer to the answers than his nephew did.

Lord, give them both clear minds and clear hearts, she prayed as she remembered them both. *Please make a path for them, and help them to stay on it. Protect them from heartache.*

She took a deep breath and continued praying for her husband and family. She prayed for her good friend Hannah, now out of town to look after her mother-in-law, who had suffered a broken hip after a fall. And then she remembered some of the women she knew from church.

Charlotte might have continued like this for some time had she not been startled from her prayers by the sound of crisp footsteps in the leaves—deliberate yet quick enough for her to recognize them as her husband's.

And so she snapped open her eyes while holding onto the remains of the stillness she'd settled into during the past half hour. Though several trees now shielded her from view, Bob would see her in a moment, and she waited for him to notice.

But he didn't, though Charlotte was hard to miss in the early morning sun that now filtered through trees and had begun to light the gully. She thought of calling out his name, but chose instead to wait, her finger still parked on those verses from the psalm. She waited as Bob walked right up to the stream, not ten yards from where she sat.

He knelt as if to get a drink, dipped his hands in the moving waters, and splashed his face and head. Even this early in the day, and even at this time of year, she knew how her farmer husband could work up an honest sweat.

But something else was obviously bothering him as he straightened up again. As he looked around the glade, Bob rubbed his eyes and squinted, shaking his head slightly. He even seemed to look straight at Charlotte for a brief moment, and he paused but didn't acknowledge her.

"Bob?" Finally she couldn't remain silent any longer, and he started at the sound. "Over here."

At least his hearing was still good. He wiped his wet hands on the tail of his shirt as he finally stepped over to join her.

"Didn't see you sitting there," he told her. "You're too quiet."

"You stared right at me. Are you all right?"

He blinked his eyes and gave his head that slight shake once again.

"You know how it is. A little dark in here under the trees. You were hard to see, sitting over here on the log."

Charlotte wasn't sure how he could say that, with the bright rays of October sunlight now illuminating the glade like a cathedral. A little dark? She looked at him more closely, but his face offered no clues. Knowing him, though, he would probably hurry back to his work, the way he had been doing so often lately. She closed the Bible and took a deep breath as she stood, stretching her legs.

"Actually," she told him, "there's something I've been meaning to talk to you about."

As quickly as she dared, she related what Pastor Evans had asked her, adding as much as she could about the young couples' seminar, what a help it would be, and how much everyone was looking forward to it. All the while she could see Bob's face clouding over as he realized what he was being asked. She had expected as much, only perhaps not quite to this degree. Finally she paused to get his response.

Bob jammed his hands in the pockets of his work jeans and frowned.

"You're saying he wants us to talk to them?" he asked. "Wouldn't it be better if *he* talked to 'em?"

"No, that's the point, dear. He wants someone else's viewpoint. A couple who's been married some years. Someone like us."

Still he frowned. "You know I don't talk in public like that. He knows it too, for that matter."

"I know, dear. But we could always try something new, don't you think? I mean, after all these years. You sound like an . . . well, like an old man."

"Seems to me that's what most people think I am anyway."

"Oh, Bob. You know what I mean. I think it would do us both some good to meet with some young couples. We would just tell them our stories, that's all. I'm sure you could do that. And I think it would be an interesting experience for both of us."

"Speak for yourself. Why are you pushing it so hard?"

"I just think it would be nice to get involved, that's all. You never know when you might actually like something, unless you step out, right? And since we were asked, I'd really like to—"

She paused as Pete's voice drifted toward them, calling for his father.

"I don't think so, Char," Bob shook his head. "You tell the pastor he probably needs to find someone else."

"You're going to say no, just like that?"

"Down here, Pete!" He yelled back, giving their son a homing signal.

Charlotte sighed, though for the past several days she'd been expecting this kind of response from her husband. Why else had she been delaying the question? Still, he'd said "probably," which technically left the door open a tiny bit. There just had to be some way to make him reconsider.

"I'm not going to tell him no," she finally blurted out. "Not just yet."

Bob's shoulders slumped as he turned away, and she decided to risk coming at it from a slightly different direction. By now she felt as if she were badgering him, but so be it.

"Can't we just think about it a little more?" she asked. "Maybe even pray on it."

Well, that stopped him in his tracks, but this time he didn't turn around as Pete called out once more, much closer.

"You pray on it if you like, Charlotte," Bob told her, and she could tell he was measuring his words carefully this time. "Then maybe we'll see if the Lord goes and tells us the same thing. But I'll say right now, I don't have anything to tell these young couples, even if I wanted to get up there in front of them all and make a fool of myself."

It wasn't like her husband to use the Lord's name lightly, and this was no different. As Pete stepped down into the glade she knew that was the end of the conversation. Toby nipped at his heels and barked her hello when she discovered Charlotte, her favorite human.

"There you are!" Pete smiled his own hello. "I was wondering where you guys had run off to."

"Didn't run off nowhere," snapped his dad, striding by in the opposite direction. "And I got plenty of work to do, just like you."

Pete gave his father a puzzled sideways glance but waited a moment for Charlotte to collect her things and catch up.

"What's gotten into him?" Pete asked in a small voice.

Charlotte hesitated a moment, not wanting to get Pete involved.

"Let me guess," he said as they walked slowly back toward the house, Toby again at their heels. "Pastor Evans asked you to speak to the young couples' retreat, and Dad said he doesn't want to."

"That doesn't sound like a guess to me," she answered. "Who have you been talking to?"

"You can hear Dad bellowing a mile away. I heard every word he was saying. 'Don't want to make no fool of myself.'"

He did a pretty fair imitation of his father's voice, though it didn't sound entirely respectful.

"You shouldn't speak about your father that way. He doesn't bellow."

"Sorry. But you know how Dad is. You sure you want him to stand up in front of everybody, with a spotlight in his eyes?"

"Now you're exaggerating, Pete. It really wouldn't be

that bad. After all, it's just for a few young couples, like you and Dana."

He sort of flinched. She hadn't meant to embarrass him.

"Anyway, the point is . . ." She did her best to smooth over the comment. "How often do we get a chance to do something like this? It's really nonthreatening."

"Yeah, nonthreatening to whom?"

She gripped her Bible a little more tightly, wondering if she had pushed her husband too far this time or if she should have just let the matter drop.

"I'll be surprised if he does it, Mom." Pete shook his head. "There's no way."

Unfortunately, her son was probably right. Charlotte sighed and looked back at their land, past the glade where Heather Creek wound through the property, and east toward the cornfields and the rising sun. Another beautiful sunrise. And in a picture-postcard moment, the sun's rays glinted off a rusty metal wing of the old windmill, framing it in the distance.

Chapter Eight

Designed to place free, limitless wind generation into the hands of farmers and rural landowners on a scale never before seen..."

The video's narrator sounded convincing enough as Pete joined the small cluster of farmers gathered around a portable TV screen at AA Tractor Supply the next morning. A couple of men glanced away just long enough to give Pete a quick nod of hello, and then turned their attention back to the show. For now, it was pass-the-popcorn time.

"In partnership with South-Central Nebraska Power and Light," continued the smooth-talking announcer, "TurboGen LLC will research your land's suitability and then provide you with a complete, no-obligation written evaluation before setting up one—or several—TurboGen6000 wind power generation towers. Our professional team will handle all the technical issues of wiring and connecting to the local power grid, ensuring a completely safe and trouble-free installation. They'll work with you and with local government on any siting or permitting issues. And best of all, we'll pay for all installation costs, leaving nothing to chance. All you have to do is enjoy the benefits of going green, and then collect the green you receive as part of the TurboGen Power Grid Percentage Program. It's never been easier."

The program ended with another beautiful shot of three new white windmills turning slowly in the middle of a waving field of corn while patriotic strains played in the background.

A young man turned off the TV as he rubbed his hands together and looked around at the assembled group.

"So," said the young man, wiping the back of his hand across his sweaty forehead, "are there any questions before I tell you a little more about the TurboGen6000?"

"Yeah." Walt Freeman raised his hand from the back of the room, over by the twirling display of Chilton shop manuals. "How good are these things at chasing crows away?"

The other half-dozen guys chuckled at the joke, but it only seemed to make the young man squirm even more than before. Of course, in his white shirt and dark blue tie, he already looked more than out of place.

"Uh, well, actually we don't have any figures on that, not exactly. However . . ." He slipped a couple of fingers beneath his collar and yanked, as if trying to catch his breath while his Adam's apple worked and he swallowed. "We do have a study going on right now at the U of N to show that local wildlife, livestock, and birds are not adversely afflicted . . . affected. You know."

"You mean my bird dog won't chase this thing?" asked Walt, and again the boys chuckled as they watched to see how the uncomfortable young salesman would react to their gentle ribbing. By this time Pete was actually feeling a little sorry for the salesman though. The kid probably wasn't even out of college yet, or if so, just barely.

"Actually," he replied, "it's perfectly safe. Depending on the installation, the blades are at least twenty feet off the ground, so you can't reach them—and neither can your animals."

The fellow went on with his memorized presentation, pointing to a stand-up display he'd perched on the counter and handing out colorful brochures featuring graceful windmills and tables of technical information that few of them probably understood.

"What I want to know is . . ." Walt interrupted the presentation once more. "How much money would this thing make us? You been up to my field, and you've seen the neighbor's place. But the way I understand it, your company drops this thing on my property and then takes most of the profit, right?"

"Glad you asked, Mr. Freeman." The young man finally brightened a little as he pointed to some numbers on his display. "Because as you can see, our return on investment . . ."

He went on with a load of figures and percentages. As far as Pete could understand, though, the bottom line was that each landowner would stand to earn 2 or 3 percent of the profits generated from one of these high-tech generators. But in an economy where high interest rates, soaring operating costs, and low commodity prices were strangling the farm's everyday profits, maybe a couple bucks here and there wouldn't hurt.

In fact, if they could get a few of these windmills spinning up on the North Quarter rise, maybe that would help their bottom line. After all, if he couldn't keep Heather Creek Farm going, how could he ever expect Dana to marry him? Maybe if she saw that he was willing to try something new, well, maybe she would be a little more willing to jump into all the uncertainty the farm represented.

"Right, Pete?" Brad Weber's question brought him out of his daydream with a jerk, but he didn't want to admit he'd tuned out.

"Uh, sure, Brad. If you say so."

That seemed to satisfy Brad, who nodded as the earnest young man wrapped up his pitch. But by this time Pete noticed eyes starting to glaze as the rest of the guys excused themselves one by one and slipped away. Work to do, you know. Fields to harvest. After five more minutes of mind-numbing technospeak the only ones left were Pete, the TurboGen guy, and of course Brad, who was still trapped behind the counter.

"So what do you think?" the salesman finally paused and turned to Pete. "We could begin a feasibility study for your property right away, maybe have a generator or two up in a few months. Mr. Freeman was kind enough to let me do some preliminary checks on his property, and the area shows promise."

Pete looked around and backed up a step, just in case the guy might be talking to someone else.

"You talking to me?"

He should have slipped out with the other guys when he had a chance, he thought.

"Well, sure," said the salesman. "All you do is fill out a

preliminary application, and we'll take it from there. Nothing to it."

The young man smiled and extended a clipboard toward Pete, who couldn't help noticing the guy's hand was shaking. And it made him wonder: What would happen if this kid returned to his bosses without at least one agreement?

"No obligation then?" Pete just wanted to be sure.

"None at all. You have the option at any time before the final agreement to change your mind, and everything depends on the outcome of our site evaluation. Here, let me show you some of the tables that explain how—"

"No, actually, that's okay." Pete took the outstretched clipboard and unfastened the form. "Let me just take this home with me. Can I mail it back to you?"

The young man's face dropped a little, but he recovered quickly.

"Sure. If you'd rather do it here, though, it really only takes a minute. I can help you get it done before you leave, and we can work through the approval process that much quicker."

"No need." By this time Pete knew he just had to get out of there, so he stuffed the application into the pocket of his jacket and held out his hand. "Good to meet you, though, er..."

"Justin." The salesman extended a business card with one hand while he shook Pete's with the other. "Justin Landwehr. Can I give you a call in a couple of days?"

"Actually, no. I'll get back to you. I need to check this out with my dad before we go ahead with anything. But thanks a lot." Pete patted the application and nodded at Brad before turning away to leave.

"You need anything else, Pete?" Brad wanted to know. "How's that old combine of yours holding out? Heard the Museum of Antique Farm Machinery in Lincoln wanted it for a display."

"Very funny." Pete shook his head with a smile and went along with the ribbing. "Actually I do need a part for that combine; that's what I came for, after all."

Pete told Brad exactly what he needed, made his purchase, and then headed out of the store toward his truck.

"So you gonna be a wind farmer, Pete?" Walt passed him from behind. "Quite a deal, huh? Looks like they'll buy you a cup of coffee every three months if you let 'em put up their mills on your property."

"Actually," Pete answered, "I could use a cup of something hot right about now."

Walt just kept walking in the direction of Herko's Market. Pete looked back inside AA, where the windmill man was folding up his stuff. He jammed his hands into the pockets of his grease-stained work jacket and leaned against the wind that was supposed to bring them so much power.

What could be so wrong with a windmill? Maybe Dana would think it was a good idea. Maybe she would be impressed with him for being innovative and forward thinking. Maybe she would want him to turn the entire farm into a model wind farm, and they could get rid of their old tractors once and for all.

The more Pete thought about the idea, the more he liked it. He hurried to his truck, hoping it would start, and pointed it toward the high school.

He turned the radio up as he cruised slowly by the school, wishing like a lovesick high schooler that he might catch a glimpse of Dana through one of the windows. He couldn't help asking himself the same question over and over.

Why in the world would she ever want to marry a hayseed like me? All I can offer the lady is a farm full of broken machinery, a pile of debts, and a pitiful bank account.

Chapter Nine

"All right, ladies and gentlemen, let me have your attention, please." Mr. Anderson was always saying that, mainly because the kids in first-period sociology 301 at Bedford High School rarely paid attention to their teacher. If they did, it wasn't very much. Not even after Mr. Anderson clapped his hands, which did little to wake Todd Moody, who sat next to Sam, two seats from the back of the room.

The thing about Todd was that he could sleep with his eyes open—a skill Sam envied him. And at the moment, Todd was employing that skill to his best advantage. Even so, Sam knew his teacher would keep talking, no matter what.

"I want us to be working on our school-to-work folders these next few weeks, since they're due when, Mr. Slater?"

"End of the semester," Sam replied without hesitation. Todd woke up enough to whisper, "Excellent, Mr. Slater," just a moment before their teacher said the same thing, like an anticipated echo.

Excellent, Mr. Slater. But not so excellent was the fact that Sam was no closer to completing the assignment than he had been a month ago. And since this was one of the classes he shared with Arielle Friesen, Sam was determined to make a good showing in class, staying awake where Todd fell asleep. No matter what, he was going to try to pay attention as much as possible, even if he had stayed up late the night before. Even if it meant actually listening to Mr. Anderson's sleep-inducing lectures on human development, social institutions, and behavioral changes. Even if it killed him or incapacitated his brain. He would take the worst Mr. Anderson and sociology 301 could dish up, all for the chance to sit a few feet away from Arielle.

Without moving his head he kept track of Arielle's perfect nose, her perfect hair, and the perfect way she sat behind her desk. She probably earned the only A-plus in the class, since the other twenty-six kids were only there because sociology was required for graduation or they had thought it was going to be an easy pass/fail. No such luck. Funny thing was, Arielle didn't seem to notice how much she stood out from the crowd, and he meant that in a good way. Maybe that kind of cluelessness made her all the more attractive in a class full of dorks.

"I'm glad you remember when this is due." Mr. Anderson erased a stray blue scribble on his whiteboard before lumbering back to his desk to pick up a bright pink binder. With a theatrical flourish he held it in the air for all to see. "So let me show you what we're talking about, ladies and gentlemen. This is what I want to see from all of you."

Here it comes. Sam had a pretty good idea whose school-to-work folder was on display when he glanced over at Arielle, whose cheeks had turned a shade of pink to match the binder. But she said nothing as their teacher exalted the value of neat organization, topic dividers and tabs, a thorough table of contents, and all the other stuff he liked.

"Here's where this student has documented her volunteer work in the counseling office," he told them, walking around with the binder so they could see neatly mounted snapshots across two pages, with captions printed underneath. "She also worked in last spring's flood-relief efforts, so there are a couple of paragraphs about that; she's volunteered at the Bedford Gardens Convalescent Center, and there's a description of how she worked at her church's food pantry as well. Plus photos. Can everybody see that?"

By this time Arielle was slumping just a bit in her chair, and Sam couldn't blame her. Obviously everyone knew what was going on—and really it wasn't the first time Arielle's work had been shown off as an example. But Mr. Anderson was really milking it this time.

"Oh, and here's the page where she's included copies of her college applications—four of them, actually—including the University of Nebraska, where she hopes to major in social science and eventually enter the workforce as a social worker. Correct so far, Miss Friesen?"

Oh, man. Mr. Anderson had to be a certified expert in embarrassing the socks off his students. Arielle barely managed to squeak out an answer as their teacher asked for questions. But by that time Todd Moody had awakened from his latest nap, and he raised his meaty hand.

"What if we already know what we're going to do, and it's not college?"

"You already know, huh?" Mr. Anderson finally set Arielle's binder back down on his desk, adjusted his rimless glasses, and gave Todd a questioning look.

"Yeah. I'm going to drive a truck for my Uncle Bill in Lincoln. He doesn't care if I go to college or not. He doesn't care about my school-to-work folder."

"*Hmm.* I suppose you asked him? Well, it doesn't matter if you're planning on college or not. This is simply a good tool to help you hone the skills you'll need, no matter what. This is what I told you last week. Now take Mr. Slater, for example . . ."

Great, thought Sam, *here it comes.*

Sam gripped the sides of his desk, as if bracing for impact. Mr. Anderson was going to pick on him again.

"Do you have any idea what you might like to do with your life?"

Except for the clicking clock on the wall, the classroom fell silent as everyone turned to see what Sam would say. Even Arielle looked at him, so he straightened up and cleared his throat. Better come up with something highly intelligent and totally impressive.

"Uh . . ." He searched his brain for the right words, but came up blank. "I was sort of thinking I could maybe do something with software development."

"Maybe something lwith software development." Mr. Anderson repeated the comment, which sounded very lame coming from an adult. "Well, that's a definite maybe. Anything else? Any plans you'd like to share? Because I haven't seen them yet in your school-to-work folder. Actually, I haven't seen anything in your school-to-work folder. What about your higher education?"

"Higher? I don't know. Depends on if I can get a soccer scholarship someplace."

"Soccer," Todd whispered in a sort of falsetto, "the sport for real men."

That brought a giggle from a handful of football players in that part of the room and a stern look from Mr. Anderson, who probably had not heard the remark.

"Well, if that's what you want to do, Sam, you're going to have to get going on your folder. As I said, I haven't seen a single page yet. And the bad news is I can say the same for at least half the class. You know who you are. What are you doing, saving it all up for the night before the due date? You know you're not getting out of this class without a completed project, so I suggest you all get busy. Do I make myself clear?"

Apparently he did, and abundantly so, as Sam heard no further smart remarks from any of the other guys around him. He managed to survive the rest of the class by flying under Mr. Anderson's radar, letting everyone else answer his questions, and generally acting pretty much just like Todd Moody and the jocks in the back of the room. Cool and detached. The strategy probably would not attract Arielle's attention, but at least it got him through to the bell.

Only problem was, Arielle seemed in an awfully big hurry once they got out into the hall, and Sam practically had to run to keep up with her on the way to her locker.

"Hey, Arielle!" he called out, dodging through a crowd of girls and almost knocking into one. "Wait up!"

She did, but he wasn't sure he liked the look on her face when she finally finished turning her combination and yanked open her locker, as if he'd said something to hurt her feelings.

"Mr. Anderson was sure embarrassing you back there, huh?"

Maybe that was it. Girls got upset at the strangest things. She looked away and placed her books one by one into her neatly organized locker.

"Hey." He rested his hand on her locker door, just in case she was going to slam it shut and run off. "You okay?"

"Sure." She didn't look it by the way she pressed her lips together and still wouldn't look at him. Her face was kind of red, like it had been when Mr. Anderson had been putting her on the spot. Maybe she was still upset about that.

"Ari?" Now what should he say? That he was sorry for something? Could it have been his fault?

"I have to go, Sam. I'm going to be late for class."

No, she wasn't. They still had a couple of minutes, and her next class was just two doors down. Sam knew he was probably pushing his luck, but he didn't let go of her locker door until she finally looked back at him with her piercing blue eyes. Goodness. His knees wobbled, and right then he knew he would probably agree to go rob a bank, if she asked him.

Good thing she didn't. Finally she slumped her shoulders, as if she were giving in.

"It's really none of my business, Sam."

"What? Would you quit being so mysterious? What's none of your business? Was it Mr. Anderson? Come on."

She sighed. "It's not Mr. Anderson."

"Then what? What did I do?"

"You didn't do anything, exactly. It's just that you're smarter than that, Sam! Don't you see? I know you're not as dense as all those . . ." She looked around to see who stood near them in the hall. "As those jocks in sociology class."

"Oh, is that it? I didn't mean to—"

"So why did you make yourself sound that way?"

"Uh . . ." Sam stepped back from the unexpected force of Arielle's words. Now he really didn't have any way to defend himself. "What did I say?"

"That's just it! You didn't say anything! Mr. Anderson was asking what you're interested in, and you didn't say any of the things you've told me. Nothing about your dreams or all the things you want to do. Nothing about your flying lessons or any of that. Why not? You make him think you're . . . oh, forget it. Now I'm really late."

"Wait a minute." Sam caught her by the arm, trying not to squeeze too tightly. "I don't care what Mr. Anderson thinks."

"Well, you should. Now I really have to go."

Sam released his grip and watched helplessly as the bell rang and the prettiest girl in Bedford High hurried away from him.

"See you at lunch?" he asked. But she either didn't hear or ignored him. As the hallway cleared, all he could do was stand there by Arielle's locker, her disappointed words ringing in his ears.

But really, it was still true: all he cared about was what Arielle thought of him. He thought he'd proved to her he was motivated when he went out for the Harding soccer team. Maybe he'd never be able to please her.

Never mind. If Sam didn't hurry to his next class, he'd get another tardy. Maybe he already had one. And what would Arielle think of that?

Chapter Ten

Friday was movie day at the Bedford Gardens Convalescent Center, but that probably meant little to Bud Harbinger. Charlotte knew that as she changed the water in Greta's vase and clipped the ends off the nearly spent red carnations. They might last just another day or two.

As she replaced the vase she prayed quietly, even as she wondered what to pray for an arthritic older woman whose husband no longer knew who he was, and who no longer recognized the people he had loved all his life. Was this how life ended—so cruelly?

Dear Lord, she prayed, *what can I do here? Where is the faithfulness Greta talked about?*

She still had no idea, really, but she tidied the arrangement.

"Will Bud want to watch the film?" she asked Greta, who was sitting in her usual chair, knitting something for her grandchildren. It was always for her grandchildren. Greta looked up from her work with that sweet smile of hers, which betrayed no hint of bitterness.

"He might enjoy it some other time, but..." She looked over in the direction of her husband. He sat propped up on his bed, chin down, eyes closed, dressed in red jogging sweats and fuzzy suede slippers. Every so often he snored like an idling, ancient chainsaw, and his head bobbed slightly.

"I understand." Charlotte didn't want to be the one to wake him. "It's *Casablanca*. You know, with Ingrid Bergman and Humphrey Bogart."

That seemed like a silly thing to say; everyone knew Bergman and Bogart. But Greta nodded dutifully, as if Charlotte had just told her something entirely new, and said, "The nurse told me he didn't sleep very well last night. Perhaps that's why he's so sleepy today."

Perhaps he wasn't the only one, judging by the light turnout for the film. Charlotte glanced out the open door of Mr. Harbinger's room to see that only two older women sat in their wheelchairs in front of the big-screen TV, faces turned toward the black-and-white classic. Meanwhile, one of the young activity assistants loaded kernels into one of those theater-style popcorn poppers—probably enough popcorn to feed thirty more moviegoers.

As the smell of popcorn wafted down the hall she heard piano music from Rick's Café Américain.

Greta looked up from her knitting and smiled again. Her gnarled fingers paused and her clouded eyes held a far-off look.

"I was a teenager when Bud took me to see that movie," she recalled. "I felt like a queen. And all the girls I knew wanted to be Ingrid Bergman."

"Didn't we all?" Though Charlotte had to be a good

twenty-five years younger than Greta, still she could identify. "You must have been young."

The distant smile never left her face. "Bud was just a few years older than me. A real GI Joe, so handsome in his army uniform. Big shoulders, and a smile that made me swoon. And he noticed, all right. But it wasn't easy, right after the war."

Her voice trailed off; perhaps other memories were not as pleasant. The postwar years could not have been a good time, and of course especially difficult in Germany. Charlotte didn't press for more as she picked up some of the completed knitting on the table next to Bud's bed. Greta's story reminded Charlotte of Ruth Blake, a former resident of Bedford Gardens who had also married an American serviceman after the war.

Charlotte nodded toward Greta's knitting project. "This looks like a very nice . . . er, is it for someone in particular?"

"For my great-granddaughter Morgan in St. Louis. They tell me that's a girl's name too, though at first I wasn't sure. Now I think it's cute. I don't know if girls these days wear stocking caps, but they still need to keep warm in the winter, don't they?"

"Of course they do. I'm sure she'll be very pleased with it."

Their conversation continued like that for a while as Bogie recited his lines in the background: from great-grandchildren (Greta and Bud had three so far) to church (the Harbingers were lifelong Lutherans but lately Greta had a difficult time attending) and everything in between.

Charlotte shared a little about what her own grandchildren were doing, then finally noticed the photo album on the corner of Bud's bed.

"May I?" She reached over to pick it up while Greta nodded her permission.

"The doctor told me to keep it here by the bed. He said Bud might want to look at it sometime, that it could help him, or perhaps keep his mind going."

"That seems like a very good idea."

Greta sighed and nodded. And for the first time Charlotte thought she saw the deeper sadness in her eyes.

"I don't know, actually." Greta pulled out a few stitches. "I suppose it couldn't hurt."

Charlotte kept her emotions in check but felt her heart breaking for this faithful woman, who spent so many hours here at the convalescent center, knitting or reading, just spending time with the husband who hardly recognized her—if he did at all.

What if it were me? For an awful moment she imagined Bob on the bed instead of Bud. And then she couldn't help imagining herself in the unattractive red-vinyl easy chair next to the bed, knitting and reading out loud, tending to the man she loved. She honestly didn't know if she would stand up under the strain as well as Greta appeared to.

Don't think like that, Charlotte told herself as she gently turned the brittle pages of the photo album. On each page, scallop-edged prints had been carefully affixed with corner mounts. She paused at a wedding photo featuring a much younger Bud in his army uniform, with thick, dark hair and the steely but sure smile of a young man with his whole life ahead of him. Next to him Greta beamed in her beautiful gown and veil.

"Look there." Greta pointed to her graying photograph. "Is that my wedding photo? I'm sorry, but I can't see that clearly anymore. I have to hold it up almost right in front of my face."

Charlotte held the album closer as Greta squinted.

"You look lovely," Charlotte told her. "And I think I recognize that church in Harding. Our Savior's Lutheran?"

"That's the one. Bud's family attended there. It was actually our second wedding." She laughed. "We had a civil wedding back in Berlin—just us—and then Bud's parents insisted on a church wedding when we arrived here in the States. I didn't mind. I was so young."

"Who's that there?" Charlotte pointed.

"Bud's sister Margaret Post, my bridesmaid. We became quite close, though I hardly knew her at the time. She moved to Florida, and passed on some years back. And do you see what else? White gloves! My mother gave me a pair of white gloves she had worn at her wedding. In fact the dress was hers too. Mend or make do, that's just how it was. You weren't born then, were you?"

"Just." Charlotte smiled.

That made Greta laugh, but softly. "You're a young one then."

"Well, I don't know. It's been awhile since anyone accused me of being young."

"But that's why you come here, isn't it? To have someone remind you how young you really are?"

Charlotte deflected the question and returned her gaze to the old photo, pointing again to the young bride.

"And you were how old?"

"Here I was eighteen. Barely eighteen. Bud had just turned twenty-two." She shook her head. "Babies. We were just babies."

Speaking of babies, the next pages in Greta's album featured a number of the young ones, and Greta was happy to point out their three children—Ellen, Andy, and Julie—born in quick succession just after the war years. There was Ellen in a stroller when they lived in town, Andy on a tricycle about to take a tumble, and Julie on a pony for her sixth birthday.

Hardworking and able, Bud had always done well for the family with his engine-repair business, despite hard times. But Greta would not speak of that. And she didn't need to see the photos clearly to describe each one in detail, adding little stories about the kids. She had them all memorized, down to the month and the exact place each picture was taken.

"But I must be boring you with all these memories," she finally said, her voice softening. "You didn't come here to listen to an old woman prattle on so."

"Oh, please don't say that, Greta. I love hearing about you and your husband, your children . . ." She glanced over to see how Bud was doing, and caught her breath to see him wide-eyed and awake, quietly taking it all in. Greta noticed it then too.

"We didn't mean to wake you, dear." She set down her knitting and leaned over to pat him on the hand. "Do you need anything? Something to drink? The girls made popcorn out there. Smell that? You always like popcorn."

"I'll get him some." Charlotte started to rise, but he stopped her as he looked more closely at the photo album, as if he knew what it was. So she paused, turning back to the first pages and placing it on his lap.

"You were quite handsome there in your uniform," she told him, pointing to the photo of the couple on the front steps of Our Savior's. "And what a beautiful bride. Greta told me all about the wedding, about the white gloves she wore for the ceremony. You remember the ceremony? Is that your car there, in the corner of the photo?"

Perhaps that was too many questions, all at once. But again he looked at the album, as if for the first time. With his finger he traced a line from the old car to the couple, and back again. He muttered something about having to get the darn old Plymouth fixed, something about a flat tire.

But then he gazed up into his wife's eyes with a sudden look of knowing that Charlotte had never seen before. He looked down at the page once more, as if to double-check, and then back at Greta.

"She was very pretty, wasn't she?" Charlotte thought she would try one more time.

"She's still pretty," he whispered, and it was the clearest, sweetest thing Charlotte had ever heard from him.

Greta reached over to take his hand, and he didn't turn away.

"I'll be getting that popcorn now," Charlotte said quietly as she made for the door and closed it softly behind her.

But she couldn't help looking back through the little observation window to see two people who still loved each other very much, holding each other's hands, with tears streaming down both their faces.

"Hey, Mrs. Stevenson!" The worker who had poured so much popcorn into the popper noticed Charlotte stepping out into the hall. "I didn't know you were still here."

"Still here." Charlotte pulled a tissue out of her apron pocket and dabbed at her eyes before anyone noticed. "Just, ah, getting some popcorn for Mr. Harbinger."

"Oh yeah, he always eats a ton." Jessica, the twenty-something, swallowed a mouthful of popcorn and focused right back on the movie as she spoke.

Charlotte stood for a moment in front of the screen, watching the actress that Greta had admired so much when she was young. Jessica kept up her running commentary.

"Yeah, this movie always gets me too."

Charlotte nodded and dabbed her eyes again, still thinking of the other couple in the room behind her. Humphrey Bogart had nothing to do with it, actually.

"Then you've seen this before."

"Oh, yeah. Like five times. I've got it totally memorized. But hey, Mrs. Stevenson, I almost forgot to mention. I heard something about you speaking at the couples' retreat at church in a couple of weeks."

Charlotte was caught off guard by the comment and didn't have a good comeback. That didn't deter Jessica from continuing, however.

"So me and my boyfriend—well, Alan's my fiancé now really—we were thinking of going, since my friend Amie said she was going to go too, and we thought it would be cool to hear somebody like you with a lot of, you know, wisdom? Any idea what you're going to say?"

Charlotte stepped over to the popcorn popper, scooped out a bag for Bud, and handed it back to Jessica. Ingrid Bergman's doe-eyed expression filled the screen while the two residents in their wheelchairs followed every move.

"Would you please run this in to Mr. Harbinger in a little while? I told them I would, but I have to go."

"Uh, sure." Jessica took the bag with a puzzled look.

"Only not now. Don't disturb them. But in a few minutes."

Charlotte turned and hurried across the small lobby to the front door. She grabbed her coat from a hook and paused for a moment, still fighting back tears that blended with far too many emotions to keep track of.

The only person who has a right to talk to young people about marriage, she thought, was sitting back in that room.

"And no," she said without turning around. "I have no idea what I would say."

Chapter Eleven

Christopher fussed with his shoelaces by the back door, waiting for Grandma to finish reminding him about his Saturday chores that still needed doing. "The chicken coop hasn't been cleaned for a long time," she said, "so after lunch I'd like you to..."

If he didn't do something soon, his friend Dylan would have to spend the rest of Saturday morning sitting inside at the kitchen table, eating cookies and twitching and blinking his eyes in that peculiar way of his. So Christopher looked for Grandma to take a breath, and then took his chance.

"Sorry to interrupt, Grandma." He spit out the words as quickly as he could. "But can we go outside for just a couple of minutes? I want to show Dylan something."

Grandma looked at him as if he were about to break another rule or do something extremely rude.

"I promise not to go near the creek," he added, holding up his hand in a Boy Scout salute. "And we won't rip our pants on barbed wire, get our hands caught in any power tools, or even touch the tractor."

Maybe he shouldn't have mentioned the tractor.

"We, we promise." Dylan echoed Christopher's words with a labored puff of air and a shrug of his shoulders. With all his extra movements and twitches and stuff, it took Dylan twice as long to say anything. Their teacher once told Christopher that Dylan had something like Tourette's syndrome, only different. But Christopher really didn't care, not like a lot of the other kids at school who acted afraid of Dylan or made fun of him when they thought he wasn't looking. He just thought Dylan was fun to be around, after you got used to all the twitching and funny noises.

"Oh, I'm not worried about that, Dylan." Still Grandma hesitated. "I just promised your mother I'd keep an eye on you until she comes back from Harding."

Dylan just nodded and looked at her with his sparkly dark eyes, which seemed like they could see right through things. He'd once told Christopher he got his eyes from his Dakota Sioux and Winnebago grandparents. Christopher just thought it would be cool someday to look different, with honey-colored skin and dark hair.

"All right, then. Why don't we do this?" Grandma went to a cupboard and pulled out a couple of little handheld walkie-talkies. "The men sometimes use these to keep track of each other out in the field, where there's no cell phone service. Here, I'll keep one with me. Christopher, you take the other one. I'll call you when it's time for Dylan to go."

"Sure thing, Grandma!"

Christopher wasn't wasting any time; he whisked his friend out the back door before Grandma could change her mind. And once they had found their freedom on the back porch, Christopher sprinted toward the barn and beyond.

"Come on!" he told Dylan, kicking up gravel as he ran and getting a head start. With Dylan, he would need it. "It's out this way."

"This way" meant around the far side of the big barn, past the chicken coops, and then straight to the far hill. Never mind that they'd both neglected to wear their jackets in the cool morning. In their hurry to escape, it didn't matter, not even if it rained or hailed. And besides, Dylan could run just as fast as Christopher could—twitches or no twitches.

So Christopher pointed up at the rise and the old windmill as they climbed together, slowing down a bit as they neared the top.

"My great-great-great grandpa put this here," explained Christopher, pointing up at the remains of the old windmill. "Or maybe it was just great-great. Anyway, it's my secret spot, and I'm going to fix up the windmill someday. Maybe hook it up to a generator. Then we can have lights and stuff out here in our fort."

"A fort? Cool. So it's okay with your grandpa if we build it out here?"

"Sure." Christopher nodded. "We can even put it up off the ground, like a treehouse. See, we'll use the four legs for the four corners. You know, with windows and a porch and a trapdoor."

"And a rope ladder!"

"Yeah, I thought of that too. But look here." He bent down by one of the tower corners and pointed to a string stretched along the ground. "I've even got a burglar alarm."

"What do you need that for?" Dylan touched the string gingerly.

"Oh, you know. If anybody comes too close to our secret place, the alarm will go off and we'll know about it." He demonstrated by plucking the string with his toe.

"Yikes!" Dylan winced as he clamped his hands over his ears at the piercing tone. "Turn it off!"

Christopher had done this before. He found the end of the string, attached to a small pin that plugged right back into the side of the battery-powered buzzer hidden behind one of the windmill's four steel legs. There.

"Pretty loud, huh?" said Christopher.

Dylan squinted even more as he gingerly lifted his hands from his ears.

"That killed my ears," he said. "But you think you can hear it from the house if anyone comes here?"

"I don't know. Maybe. But it sure would scare people off."

They agreed on that point. But that wasn't even the best part. The best part lay hidden in the tangle of leaves and vines between the four legs of the old windmill tower. Christopher proudly pulled away an old brown-and-yellow camouflage blanket to reveal the prize. And as expected, Dylan's eyes widened with surprise.

"Where did you get that?" he asked. "It's huge."

"Didn't get it. Grew it. Grandpa gave me the seeds, and we've been watering it with chicken manure for a couple months, watching it get bigger and bigger. His name is Mr. Pumpkin."

"That's original."

"Better than nothing. I thought it would be good luck if

we named it. 'Course, there used to be more, but the rest of them died."

"So you gonna eat it?"

"Heck, no. It's for the *Bedford Leader* Giant Pumpkin Contest they have every year. Mr. Barnes is the judge, and they put your picture in the paper with your pumpkin when you win. We're going to win."

Given the size of the pumpkin, now larger than a beach ball, Dylan had no reason to doubt him.

"So what are you going to win?"

"Forty bucks for first, thirty for second, and twenty for third. Only my grandpa made me agree to—well, never mind."

Dylan flinched and whistled in admiration as they both leaned closer to examine the monster pumpkin—which would never win any beauty contests with its crusty red, orange, and gold skin. One side bulged out quite a bit more than the other, giving the impression that it was about to topple over. Scabs and scars covered its rough sides.

"I've never seen one this big," said Dylan, lowering his voice, as if he were in a cathedral. "At least not in person."

"Me neither." Christopher pulled a piece of string from his pocket and, with some difficulty, stretched it around the overweight pumpkin's girth. "It's maybe two inches bigger than it was last time I checked. But you should have seen it growing before. You could, like, stand here and just watch it grow."

Well, that was only stretching it a little. But there was no denying that their monster had a real chance of winning the annual pumpkin contest.

"How do you get it out of here?" asked Dylan.

"Grandpa's going to help me lift it. Or if it's too big, Grandpa said he would use the loader on the tractor and we'll lift it straight into the back of his truck."

"Cool," said Dylan once more, duly impressed.

By this time Christopher was feeling the chilly wind, and he couldn't help shivering. He thought maybe they should think about getting back.

"So you're the only one who comes up here, huh?" Dylan wanted to know. Christopher nodded his head.

"Me and sometimes my grandpa."

"So what's that from?" Dylan pointed to a pair of large tire tracks nearby, sunken into the mud where the vehicle had obviously run into a bit of trouble.

Christopher bent closer to see. "I'm still trying to find out," he finally admitted. "Nobody's supposed to be up here 'cept us. Grandpa said he didn't drive his truck up here, and it doesn't look like it's from Uncle Pete either."

"Maybe it's burglars."

"That's what I'm thinking."

Christopher didn't like that possibility, but he couldn't say it wasn't. He also still didn't like the idea that someone had been driving around up here by the windmill without his knowing about it. Just wasn't right. So he dug the length of string back out of his pocket and handed one end to Dylan.

"Here," he told Dylan. "I've got an idea. Tie your end to that stick over there, and poke it into the ground. I'll tie my end to the trip string that's attached to the buzzer."

Dylan smiled. "And maybe we'll catch your burglar."

"Maybe."

Christopher busied himself with their plan, and then gave the new, longer trip string a satisfied twang.

"Don't!" Dylan raised his hands to his ears once more, but Christopher only smiled.

"Don't worry. But if anybody comes snooping around, next time we'll know."

He stood up and rubbed his hands together to warm them, satisfied they'd done all they could. Dylan helped him cover the pumpkin back up with the blanket.

"Christopher?" Grandma's voice crackled over the walkie-talkie. "Are you out there? It's time for Dylan to go. He can have another cookie before he leaves."

Christopher held the radio to his mouth and pressed the talk button.

"Cookies? Coming! Over!"

CHARLOTTE WAS PLEASED that she had assembled everyone for Saturday supper, even Dana, who looked very nice in a cream blouse and pressed jeans, her dark hair pulled back in a ponytail. No matter what, she always looked like a teacher.

Charlotte smiled as she looked around the table at her brood, all in one place, and for a change no one seemed in a hurry to be anywhere else.

Before the meal Bob said the blessing and then Charlotte urged everyone to dig in. Pete didn't hold back and scooped out a large helping of mashed potatoes a few moments later as Dana watched him with a barely concealed smile.

"I think our boy is hungry." Charlotte exchanged

glances with Dana, who nodded while Pete dug into his dinner.

"So, Grandma, can we go ahead and have the harvest party I asked you about?" Emily ventured as she filled her plate with salad.

"Harvest party?" Bob asked as he glanced at Charlotte. "We haven't had one of those in years."

"I know, but Emily mentioned it and I thought it would be a great way to get everyone together," Charlotte explained. "Remember how much fun we always had at those parties—the bonfire, the s'mores?"

"Yeah, some of my friends wanted to have one," Emily said with a shrug, "but their parents wouldn't let them. So I asked Grandma."

"So you should all invite your friends next Saturday night after the game," Charlotte announced.

"Saturday?" asked Pete. "What happened to football Friday night under the lights?"

"Apparently there's some kind of benefit game Saturday, rather than Friday. So if we're going to have a harvest party after the game, it's going to have to be then. We'd like you to be here too, Pete. You and Dana both."

He glanced over at Dana. "Uh, actually, Mom, I don't know if she—"

Charlotte held up her hand to quiet him.

"I'm sure Dana can speak for herself."

"I think it sounds like a fine idea," said Dana. "I wouldn't miss it for anything."

"You wouldn't?" Pete looked surprised.

"Great. Then it's settled," Charlotte said with a smile.

"Uh, not to change the subject from bonfires and

s'mores," Pete said. "But I've been talking to a guy from TurboGen."

"Turbo-what?" Bob hadn't understood.

"TurboGen. The windmill people. You remember I mentioned it to you the other day. They want to do a feasibility study to see if our winds are right for setting up a turbine."

"You mean here at Heather Creek?"

"I mean here at Heather Creek."

"I think that sounds like an exciting idea," said Charlotte, and Dana nodded.

"*Hmm.*" Bob chewed carefully on his last bite of ham. "What's it cost us?"

"Nothing," Pete replied. "That's the deal. They put it up, and they pay for it. We get a cut from whatever profit it generates."

"Don't believe it for a second. You never get something for nothing."

"Well, you can believe it or not," Pete countered. "They're just looking for the best places around here to build their windmills. Green power, right?"

"Sounds pretty cool to me," said Christopher as Pete continued.

"I was thinking maybe up on the hill, where there's always a breeze."

"You mean up by my, er . . . by the old windmill?" Christopher asked.

"Exactly," Pete said, then turned to his father.

"*Hmm.*" Still Bob appeared less than enthusiastic. "You haven't told him yes or no, have you?"

"Not yet. I've been talking to their rep, Justin Landwehr,

about it. Real nice guy, actually. He's got all kinds of reasons we should have one sited here. He thinks it might be better than the neighbor's property, even."

"Freeman's?" That got Bob's attention. Pete nodded and went on, keeping an eye on Dana's reaction.

"Right. But I thought I'd better discuss it with you first. I could give you some stuff to read. Or not."

"Bob." Charlotte knew from experience when polite dinner conversation could go bad, and she certainly didn't want that to happen with Dana here. "Don't you think we should at least look into it? If Pete thinks it's a good thing..."

"Maybe so."

Bob wasn't softening his views for anybody—guests or no guests. Fortunately, Pete still sounded positive.

"Anyway, we can't be thinking too long, Dad. I don't know how much longer Justin's going to be in town. They're going to go with the first farms that can get their act together."

"*Hmm*," Bob repeated. "I'm not saying it's a bad idea or a good idea. I'm just saying I'll need to think on it."

Charlotte took the opportunity to start clearing the dishes.

"Well, while you men are pondering, why don't I bring out some dessert?" She winked at Dana. "Maybe you'll be able to think a little better over a slice of pie."

Chapter Twelve

Charlotte liked this time of morning, just after the kids had left for school, when Bob and Pete were still out doing their thing. Or more accurately, when Pete was out doing the work while Bob was offering advice.

In any case, this was the time when she could decide what to do—listen to music or start some chore. She yawned and rubbed her aching temples, feeling the effects of waking up at 3:00 am and not being able to get back to sleep, worrying about Bob and his vision problems. Toby looked up at her from the kitchen floor and thumped her tail.

"What, did the kids not feed you? Poor thing." She poured a bowl of dog food, which Toby put away without lifting her nose from the bottom of the dish. Which reminded her . . .

Did I see any fresh eggs this morning? She couldn't remember. *Wonder if they forgot to feed the chickens too. What else did I miss?*

Her question was answered when she noticed a hastily scrawled note pinned under a missionary prayer magnet on the front of the fridge. In the confusion of kids running in and out of the kitchen (and the plugged toilet!) she'd apparently missed that as well. So now she pulled it down and read it out loud.

sorry, g-ma, late for school gotta run. can u please feed chickens and toby this am? i'll make it up. e

Hmm. A note was all very well, she supposed, even with Emily's apparent aversion to capital letters. Still, these kids would need a good talking to when they got back from school. They knew better than to blow off their chores—even if they had almost been late for school.

With a sigh Charlotte found her faded denim work jacket and slipped it on as she stepped outside into another cool morning. The air was laden with the scents of fallen leaves seasoned with frost and a hint of distant wood smoke. An extra bit of cackling in the distance reminded her that the hens were getting restless.

"All right, girls," she told them. "Keep your feathers on. I'm coming!"

But she'd barely made it past the barn when she heard another sound—not hungry chickens, this time. Like a buzzer of some kind.

What in the world?

Only that wasn't the end of it. With a tilt of her head she zeroed in on the disturbance and determined that it had to be coming from the other side of the barn, up the rise a bit. The chickens would have to wait a little longer. She changed course to investigate.

As she did, and as the buzzer continued, she could not miss Bob's voice. Now he sputtered and fussed as only her husband could do. She doubled her pace and trotted up the rise, using the old windmill as a guide.

"What is this?" he fumed as she approached. "Stupid..."

Now she could see that he was dancing around next to the old mill, first hopping on one leg and then on the other. He'd dropped his toolbox, scattering several tools in the process. And now he bent down and tried to untangle himself from some kind of string, without much success. The alarm—if that's what it was—sounded even more loudly and persistently.

"What did you get yourself into?" she asked him, trying to raise her voice above the ruckus. She stepped up and grabbed a string that had caught on the heel of his boot.

"Some kind of darn booby trap is what it is!" he yelled back. He let her untangle the string. Funny how helpless a man could be sometimes. What would he do without her around?

But that sound! She would have clapped her hands over her ears if she could. Instead, she did what she could to discover the source of all the racket.

"Just follow the string," she told him, and it obviously led into a patch of vines she hadn't noticed before, as if someone had planted squash or pumpkin directly underneath the old windmill, between the supporting legs. She would have to find out about that, but later. Right now she looked over at Bob, who squinted in the direction of the sound, turning his head this way and that. If someone was going to find the buzzer—or whatever it was—it probably wasn't going to be Bob.

"What are you doing?" she asked. "The string?"

He shook his head and frowned.

"Can't see any string."

So she held it up to his face, plain as day, and she herself followed it to a small buzzer taped to the back of one of the windmill legs. There! She worked the duct tape loose and held it up before prying it open and pulling out one of the batteries inside.

Blessed quiet. But now Charlotte's ears still rang.

"Wow, that was an eardrum-buster," she said, handing the buzzer over to her husband. "Do you know where it came from?"

He held it up to his face a little too closely and turned it around in his hand.

"I'll be talking to Christopher about this," he said, as if he knew something Charlotte did not. Well, that was fine with her. However, something else was bothering her.

"So what happened?" she asked him.

"Nothing. I was just coming back from where Pete was running the combine, and that darn string—"

"You didn't see it, did you? Even when I held it up. And why have you been squinting so much lately?"

"Ah, just need a new set of reading glasses is all."

"I don't think so, Bob. Pete's noticed it too when you're out working. This is more than just needing a new set of reading glasses."

"Look, Char. I can see fine enough. And if I need to read the fine print, I'll ask you."

But Charlotte wasn't satisfied with that kind of answer and she wasn't going to let him shrug this off, though she felt almost as upset with herself for not picking up on the clues over the past several weeks.

"Been getting worse the last month or two," he finally admitted. "Thought it was just, you know, the usual old age stuff."

"Robert Stevenson! I'm going to make you an eye appointment with Dr. Standish, and we're going to get this taken care of. There's no reason for you to pretend you're doing fine when you're not."

"Don't have time for any eye appointment. Pete and me—"

"Nonsense. Now are you going to call him, or do you want me to?"

He picked up his toolbox and headed off toward the barn.

"If you're going to be in the house..."

Well, fine then. If he wasn't going to take care of himself, she would see to it. The memory of Bud Harbinger sitting on his bed at Bedford Gardens flashed through her mind as she hurried back to the house. The chickens could wait just a little bit longer.

"Oh, by the way," she told him, hurrying to catch up. "You left a couple of wrenches back there on the ground."

If Charlotte was going to call the eye doctor for Bob, she decided she would let him find his own tools.

Five minutes later she was on the phone with Dr. Standish's office in Harding, setting up the appointment. "I've got a couple of slots late next week," the receptionist told her. "Unless you could come in this afternoon at three. I had a cancellation this morning."

"Perfect," Charlotte told her, jotting down the information on a pad by the kitchen phone. "We'll be there at three."

BACK HOME IN HER ROOM that afternoon, Emily left her backpack on her bed and slipped back down the stairs. Funny how it had been so quiet down here ever since they'd returned from school. She found Christopher in the living room, watching a dumb sitcom with a thoroughly tacky laugh track.

"Does Grandma know you're watching that dumb show?"

"*Hmm.*"

She parked herself in front of the screen, blocking his view. Naturally that got a reaction as he tried to see around her, but she moved with him.

"Well?" She wouldn't give up. "Does she?"

Finally Christopher collapsed back into the sofa with his arms crossed.

"Grandma isn't here. Now would you get out of the way?"

Not here? Emily thought for a moment, a bit confused. She had seen Grandma's car in the drive, but Grandma wasn't in the kitchen when they got home. Still Emily had assumed she was just outside doing chores.

"What about Grandpa?" she asked. "Is he out working with Uncle Pete again?"

Christopher didn't take his eyes off his stupid show.

"Huh-uh. They both went somewhere."

"When? You mean since we got home?"

"Nope."

"Oh, come on, Christopher. Did they tell you or what?"

"Note on the table."

"Why didn't you say so?"

"Just did."

Honestly, sometimes she could just scream. Instead she checked the kitchen, where a note on the kitchen table told her what her little brother could have explained, if he'd been just a tiny bit more considerate.

"Oh." She read it, "Taking Grandpa to his eye appointment. Back by dinner, but don't need to wait for us."

Emily dropped the note back on the table and went upstairs to call Ashley and make plans for the harvest party on Saturday.

IN HARDING, CHARLOTTE LEAFED through a dog-eared copy of *Good Housekeeping* as she waited for Bob to emerge from his checkup.

What's taking so long? she wondered, unable to concentrate on any of the articles. Not even the one about "Ten Secrets to a Marriage That Lasts." She avoided the receptionist's smile and instead hid behind the magazine, her mind racing.

What if he's going blind? she worried. *How will I take care of him?*

Finally she heard the exam room door open, and she peeked over the top of her magazine to see the white-frocked ophthalmologist beckoning her to join them.

"Mrs. Stevenson?" He waved her in and pointed to a chair. "It might be good for the three of us to chat."

Charlotte wasn't so sure about that, or why the doctor wanted her in on this as well. This couldn't be good. Still, she took a seat along the wall of the little room and waited. Bob sat sideways in the big exam chair in the center of the room, framed underneath the eye chart on the distant wall. He sat there, tight-lipped, with a look on his face that he reserved for bad news like extended droughts or killer hailstorms.

Thankfully, the rest of the goggle-like exam equipment had been swiveled out of the way to the far wall. The doctor had parked it there like a slumbering, long-necked dinosaur.

Dr. Standish pulled up his wheeled exam stool and sat between them, obviously trying to put on a pleasant, relaxed expression. But Charlotte had a feeling this would be neither pleasant nor relaxed.

"First of all, let me tell you the bad news, and then we'll get on to some good news." He checked the chart in his hand once again, as if speaking from notes, and then set it aside on a nearby table. "The bad news is that it appears we're well past the beginning stages of cataracts, which sounds a little ominous, I know. But let me explain what this means."

Bob sat unblinking on his chair while Charlotte reached over to rest her hand on his. Meanwhile, the doctor picked up a plastic model of an eye and went on.

"Basically, what this means is that the condition is causing your retinas, which are these areas here, to become more and more cloudy."

He sounded like a high school biology teacher Charlotte had once had, years and years ago, explaining things like viscosity and visual acuity.

"So." He turned first to Bob, and then to Charlotte. "You're following me so far?"

"You're saying I'm going blind." At times like these Bob had a way of drilling to the point. But the doctor put up his hand.

"I wouldn't put it that way, Mr. Stevenson. Not yet. We do have several options to discuss. That's where Mrs. Stevenson comes in."

"We've been trying to keep him healthy," said Charlotte, sounding as hopeful as she dared.

"That's good. Diet and medication are all very good. But because of how far this condition has advanced, I'm still going to recommend we go ahead with a simple surgical procedure, after which you're going to need to go on a much stricter diet to maintain those blood sugar levels, as well as some new medication. I'll give you a booklet that explains what we're talking about, all right?"

Charlotte nodded stiffly, but the shock was settling in. All the times lately that Bob had been struggling to see better? She should have insisted they come in before this. Maybe it would have made a difference. Maybe they could have avoided some of this.

"So hang on." Bob held up his hands. "What's the . . . what did you call it? A simple surgical procedure?"

"That's right," said the doctor, still referring to his model. "I'm recommending you for laser surgery, where we'll go in and clear this out right away. It's actually pretty common these days, and I can give you a referral to an excellent surgery center. It's an outpatient procedure. Do you understand what I'm saying?"

Bob nodded, though his expression had petrified.

"You mentioned there was good news," said Bob. "So far this sounds like a whole lotta the other kind."

The doctor finally smiled and set aside his colorful plastic eye model.

"By good news, Mr. Stevenson, I meant that we have

several courses of treatment that can prevent further vision loss. But the condition is starting to settle in, and frankly it's gone on too long. I don't mean to minimize that. It's a good thing you came in when you did."

"Wasn't me." Bob glanced over at his wife, and Dr. Standish seemed to understand.

"Well, we all need someone to spur us on sometimes, don't we?" As they all stood, he offered Bob his hand. "Now what I want you to remember is that you're in this together. All right? That's what it's going to take. No secrets."

"No secrets." Bob echoed the words under his breath.

"And I need you to remember that things are going to be a bit different from now on. Your wife here is going to have to help with your diet, the way she already has. Are you both with me there?"

They both nodded as he went on.

"So you understand this is a long-term proposition. No cheating, no shortcuts, and no sneaking a cookie when no one's looking. Right?"

If Bob had looked tight-lipped earlier, now he resembled a scolded pooch with its tail between its legs.

"We'll have a prescription for you," the doctor went on, "for a fairly new drug. We've been seeing some fairly good results, with a minimum of side effects."

Charlotte couldn't muster up the nerve to ask him what kind of side effects he was talking about, and Bob's chastised expression didn't change as the doctor went on. "Then, after your surgery, I want to see you again in a couple of weeks. Any other questions before you leave?"

They didn't have any. Dr. Standish paused at the door with his hands on their shoulders.

"All right then. If you have any questions at all, you feel free to call my office, won't you?"

Charlotte didn't know what else to say as they settled their paperwork at the reception desk, collected the literature about "Options and Cataracts," and headed out into a raw, darkening afternoon. A couple of kids flew past on their bicycles, chattering and laughing. Several crows squabbled in the bare branches of a nearly bare oak tree just overhead. Bob only looked straight ahead, as if he didn't notice any of it.

Lord, how do I encourage him? she prayed, gripping her husband's large hand and holding back when they reached the truck. She wished so desperately to say something that would ease the obvious pain, but the words only stuck in her mouth.

"I'll drive, honey," she finally told him, reaching for his keys and taking them gently from him. He would not take it as anything other than concern, would he? "Your eyes are probably feeling . . . well, I know how it is after one of those exams."

She hoped he wouldn't insist on driving, not after what the doctor had just told them. And he didn't. He just paused and looked around the parking lot. He didn't say a word, stepping around to the passenger side.

Chapter Thirteen

With some effort, Bob finished tightening the setscrew on the tractor seat the next morning. He tossed the crescent wrench back at his toolbox, missed, and sighed as he searched the meadow grass on his hands and knees.

Don't tell me I lost it again.

And no, he wasn't going to ask Pete for help, not this time.

He squinted, but that didn't seem to help much. The main problem was no light. Days had seemed so much shorter lately, and were getting shorter all the time. Who could see without light? And where had the morning sunshine disappeared to anyway?

After what the doctor had told him yesterday, he knew why his eyes had been bugging him so much lately. He understood better about the blurriness and the recent headaches, not to mention the trouble he was having seeing distant things. He just wasn't sure it helped much to know why.

As he looked around the field of half-harvested corn, he understood that maybe it didn't matter as much as he'd thought it had. He watched something flutter in the distance, some kind of bird, and saw the last golden leaves clinging to the bare branches of the cottonwoods down by Heather Creek. He could see that much.

Behind the cottonwoods, a wan autumn sun began to dip, looking almost as pretty as the leaves—blurry or not.

I've seen my share of sunsets, haven't I? he asked himself. *Soon it'll be the boy's turn to keep this place running.*

That's what his own father had told him once. But that was years ago, when Bob still had the energy to run the combine all day and then come home and fix machinery at night or reshingle the barn, all by himself.

Still, he couldn't help wishing for just a few more sunsets. Of course, if God wanted to cut his time short here on Heather Creek Farm, well, that was his business—and not Bob's to question.

Was it?

He fumbled around in the tall grass a bit more, ignoring the wet knees of his worn gray coveralls and trying not to feel like an old, blind man. A moment later his hand closed on the cold metal wrench, and with a sigh of relief he picked it up again. Over on the other side of the tractor, Pete stood staring off into space.

"Got it," Bob told him, finally picking up his toolbox and straightening back up. "You can fire up the tractor now."

Pete shook loose from his daydream and looked over at his dad, eyes wide. He looked as if he'd been napping, standing up.

"What's that?"

"I said I got it. Fixed the seat. Just a loose setscrew. Still got lots to do in this field, eh?"

"You said it. Thanks, Dad." This time Pete swung up into his mount, reaching for the starter before pausing and looking down at his dad once more. "Actually, though, can I ask you something else?"

"What, something else not running right?" Bob looked up at his grown son, who still very much looked the same as he did when he was a gangly kid of fourteen, hemming and hawing and looking at the ground sometimes when he had something serious to say.

Wonder where he got that from? Bob knew the answer as Pete's thoughts finally seemed to catch up to his words and he made a go of spitting out what was on his mind.

"I was wondering . . . ," Pete went on, looking every which way but straight at his father. "I was wondering, how did you know for sure that Mom was the one? I mean, the one you wanted to marry? How did you know?"

Oh, so that's what this is all about. Bob pointed at their tractor and spun his finger.

"Start it up, Pete. I want to show you something."

"Did you—?"

"Yeah, I heard you. Start it up. Head down toward the creek."

Pete looked at him with a startled expression but did as he was told as his father mounted the side of the tractor and found a foothold where he could stand as Pete sat and steered. The two of them rode across harvested fields of cornstalks, toward the nearby cottonwood grove where Heather Creek cut through their acres. Neither said another word until five minutes later, when Bob told him to cut the engine as they settled in under the overhanging branches of the nearest cottonwoods.

"Here's good enough," he said, hopping down to the ground. "Now follow me."

Pete did, slipping down the leaf-blanketed embankment on his father's heels. They both half-tumbled, half-slid down the little hillside, coming to a stop in a pile of pungent leaves, heavy with the signature scent of autumn. Bob got to his feet and brushed himself off, and then pointed to one of the larger trees.

"Right over there," he told Pete. "I've told you this story, right?"

"Only once or twice."

"You asked, so I'm telling. I was nervous that day. My dad asked me if I was sick or something, and as a matter of fact I asked him pretty much the same question you just asked me. How did he know my mother was the right one?"

"No kidding." A slow smile began to spread across Pete's face. "So what did he tell you?"

Bob looked up through the cottonwood branches to the pale sky beyond. A pair of crows had followed them and were squabbling somewhere just above their heads.

"He told me it was a mystery how God had prepared the right woman, only it wasn't like some guessing game he was giving me that I had to pass or fail, like there was one woman hiding somewhere in the world and I had to somehow find her or I would lose the game. You know what I'm saying? The choice was mine to make, using whatever brain the good Lord gave me."

"I'm assuming Mom had something to say about it too."

"Goes without saying."

"Just making sure. You mean it wasn't an arranged marriage?" Now Pete was pulling his leg.

"Very funny. But he said something that day I'll always remember. He asked me, 'Can you serve the Lord better with that girl, or without her? That's the question you need to answer.' So that's when I knew. Besides, I already knew I didn't want anything to do with any of the other girls I went to high school with. A lot of 'em were sort of, well, lightweights, if you know what I mean."

Now they both had to laugh, but Bob turned serious once more.

"I don't get the impression Dana's that kind of girl, is she?"

"Lightweight? No. Not at all. She's a lot like Mom."

They stood for a while, listening to the crows fussing overhead. At their feet, Heather Creek gurgled quietly. Bob didn't mind sharing the moment with his younger son. He had to admit this was a good deal easier to discuss than the birds and bees talk he'd tried, back when Pete was a teen.

"So . . . this was the place you asked Mom to marry you, right?"

"You've heard the story before."

"But not all the details. I mean, you can tell me what you want or not. I was just wondering, you know."

"All right. See that big tree over there?" Bob broke the silence as he pointed at the largest cottonwood, battered over the years and split at the top, but still proudly holding its own. "I took your mom right over there one evening in October; I remember there was a big harvest moon and I was thinking she might like to see that. I told her I didn't have much to offer, just this land that was going to be mine someday, and my own two hands. Well, more or less that's what I told her."

"But you were younger than I am right now, right?"

Bob smiled at the memory, which now seemed just a little closer as he and Pete stood here in the grove.

"By a couple years, sure. But I figured I knew the answer to my dad's question."

"The one about if you can serve God better with or without her?"

Bob nodded. "And once I knew the answer, I didn't want to waste any more time. Life is too short for messing around."

"Messing around. Is that what you think I've been doing?"

"No, I didn't mean it that way. I just meant—"

"I know, Dad. I'm just giving you a hard time. Speaking of messing around, though, maybe we should get back to work."

"I was just thinking the same thing." Bob would normally have been the first to mention it. Here in this place, though, he seemed to have lost track of time. He turned to go, not noticing the craggy finger of a cottonwood snag that hit him in the face.

"Ow!" He grunted and reeled at the pain, falling to his knees in the leaves.

"Dad!" Pete helped him to his feet. "Didn't you see that?"

"Nah, well . . . it sort of reached down and jabbed me."

"Don't know how a big tree branch like that could do such a thing, but there's a nasty scratch."

Bob ran a hand along his cheek and came back with a streak of blood. Charlotte would fuss over it, but he'd had worse. Funny how that branch had just come out of nowhere, and now his head still kind of spun from the impact. He let Pete help him up the slope to the waiting tractor.

"You know, Dad, I can actually see why they asked you to speak at the young couples' seminar. Are you going to tell them what you just told me?"

"The seminar, huh?" Bob was not at all sure how the thing he dreaded had bubbled to the surface of yet another conversation. "Your mom must be lobbying again."

"No lobbying. Wasn't even Mom who told me about it."

Then who? This whole thing with the young couples' seminar was getting ridiculous—getting up there and sharing a bunch of feelings with strangers. He shook his head to rid himself of the uneasy feeling in the pit of his stomach.

"Dad?" Pete looked back at him as he climbed the tractor. "Coming?"

"You go ahead," Bob replied, waving him off. "I'll be along."

Pete looked at him as if to ask, *Are you sure?*

"Need the exercise," Bob told Pete, still trying to get him to go. "You know, walking?"

Pete shrugged and started the tractor while Bob watched as his son disappeared through the half-harvested field.

The coughing, wheezing sound of their tractor receded in the distance under a little cloud of smoke.

"Not a chance in the world," Bob mumbled as he started out for the barn and the house beyond. He imagined people staring at him from an audience and almost started shaking. No, he figured he'd rather be locked in a stall with a wild stallion than face a roomful of people that way.

So he wiped the scratch on his cheek with the back of his hand and followed the tractor, still shaking his head.

Chapter Fourteen

"Bob! Whatever did you *do* to yourself?"

Charlotte looked with alarm at her husband's face as he dragged into the kitchen that evening, well after the dinner dishes had finished drip-drying on the rack next to the kitchen sink.

"Asked myself the same question. Sorry to miss dinner. Been a long day." Bob, seemed to be talking about something other than the gash on his cheek. He squinted at her with a sort of glazed expression reserved for the longest days of spring and fall, spent planting and harvesting. Pete hadn't yet showed up for dinner either. Had he already slipped away to his apartment? She followed Bob over to the sink, where cold water running over his rough hands turned rusty brown with the remains of a Nebraska field.

"I mean your face," she told Bob, referring to the injury that would appear so obvious to everyone but him. With his hands under the faucet, he couldn't defend himself and couldn't even back away as he usually might have done.

At first she couldn't tell how serious it was. She wet a paper towel to clean him up.

"Hey, what are you—" He started to duck, the way any one of the kids might have done, until he finally seemed to remember his injury. "Oh, that. It's nothing."

"Hold still then, and let me see. Doesn't look like nothing." She cleaned up his injury as best she could while he explained what had happened that morning.

"And you walked around all day like this?" Charlotte would have scolded him more if it would have done any good. But after all these years, she knew her man.

"Didn't hear anybody complaining," he answered. "Not until now."

"I'd hardly call this complaining, Robert Stevenson. Now you stay there while I put something on this."

Bob grumbled but held still a moment longer as she located and dabbed on some antibacterial ointment. She wondered what kind of bandage would cover such a long scratch. Fortunately it didn't appear as deep as she had first feared. Even so, Bob held up his hand for her to stop.

"No more. It's good, thanks."

By that time Pete burst in the door as he always did, ushering in a whirl of leaves and a cold draft in his wake.

"Close the door!" Charlotte told him without looking away from her work. "We don't want to be heating the entire barnyard again." She immediately gained an audience.

"I told him he should get that looked at," Pete told her as he sidled up to the operation. "That, and his eyes. He wouldn't listen to me."

"He doesn't listen to a lot of people," answered Charlotte, tightening the cap back on the ointment tube.

"*Hmm.*" Bob wiped his wet hands on a dark blue kitchen towel. "Sounds like two against one to me."

"No one's against anyone." Charlotte didn't need to turn around to know what was happening behind her in the kitchen. "And Pete, you leave that plate alone. It's for your father."

"Just looking!" Pete slammed the microwave door shut and held up his hands.

"If you wanted me to fix you something," replied Charlotte, "all you had to do was ask. You two were just out there so long, I didn't know what you were doing. And Bob, where did you get that gash anyway? Or how?"

"Tree branch," Bob explained in the fewest words possible. "Reached out. Got me."

Somehow that made Pete and Bob laugh as Bob sat down at the kitchen table to eat his warmed-over plate of mac and cheese with tuna chunks and limp broccoli. The food had appeared much more appetizing an hour or two ago, when Charlotte had first prepared it, but she donned oven mitts and slipped it in front of Bob, as is.

"Yeah." Pete chuckled again. "It reached out and got him, like those tree men in the Narnia books."

She'd read those stories to Pete and Denise when they were young, so she knew the reference. These boys apparently had no intention of sharing any more about their inside joke, however, and at this time of the evening it really made no difference to Charlotte. She crossed her arms and looked at Pete.

"So do you want me to heat you something too?" she

asked, thinking of ways to resurrect what leftovers she still might have in the fridge. "You know, meals these days would be so much easier if you boys would just let me know when we could expect you."

"Don't get too bent out of shape, Mom." Pete smiled and guided her out the kitchen door with an arm around her shoulder. "I got a frozen Mexican dinner at home I'm going to heat up. No worries."

He lowered his voice as they stepped into the living room, where Emily was doing her math homework on the couch.

"And listen, Mom, don't be too hard on Dad. I think he might be loosening up on that speaking thing."

"Loosening up?" Charlotte matched his whisper, which brought a curious look from Emily. "What exactly does that mean?"

"That means . . ." He paused as Bob looked up from his meal to see what they were conspiring about. "That means I have a few things to do tonight, so I'll see you guys later."

He did an abrupt about-face and headed for the back door, patting Bob on the back and leaving his dad with a mouthful of macaroni and a puzzled expression on his face.

"Later, Dad. I'll be waiting for you out there first thing tomorrow. The TurboGen guy's stopping by too. Take care of that injury."

"We'll see who's going to be waiting for who." Bob nodded and swallowed, nearly choking as the back door slammed shut.

"What happened to Grandpa?" asked Emily, looking up

from her schoolwork. Christopher must have heard her question, as he popped up from the sofa to see for himself.

"It's just a scratch," said Bob, waving them off. But Charlotte wasn't going to let it pass this time.

"Your grandfather had a run-in with a tree branch," she explained. "Mainly because he's been having some trouble seeing lately."

"Charlotte!" Bob started to object, but she shook her head.

"You remember what the doctor said, dear. No secrets." Again she turned to the kids. "We were at the eye doctor yesterday. Your grandfather is going to need a small operation on his eyes."

"Operation?" Christopher sounded worried. "Operations are serious."

"Not this one," countered Bob. "It's just a laser, uh, a laser *procedure*. That's all."

"It's apparently a quite common procedure," added Charlotte, "and everything's going to be fine, but we just thought you should know."

Christopher nodded, eyes wide. "But he's going to get better?"

"Oh, of course." Charlotte did her best to reassure them. "Grandpa's just not going to be driving for a while. But you don't need to worry about a thing."

"Okay." Christopher seemed satisfied as he returned to the living room. "I guess."

"I told you it was serious," Emily told her brother. She furrowed her eyebrows in concern before returning to her book while Bob went back to his dinner with a grunt. With the big announcement made and misunderstood, quiet returned to the house.

But not for long. A moment later the back door opened all over again and Pete poked his head inside. "Actually, Dad, I forgot I have a quick errand to run tomorrow morning in Harding. Feel free to get started without me. And if Justin comes by, maybe you can talk to him. 'Night."

And then he was gone the second time without waiting for his father to respond. Bob turned to Charlotte.

"Justin? Who's Justin?" Bob wondered out loud as he washed his dinner down with a gulp of cold milk. "Is that kid up to something?"

"Up to something?" Charlotte wasn't sure what he meant.

"You know, acting kind of funny. Jittery. And then he was bugging me all day about that seminar thing they want us to speak at."

Charlotte wasn't prepared to wade into the speaking controversy again, not now. Instead she opened the refrigerator and pulled out a jug of milk.

"More?"

Bob nodded his thanks as she poured him another glass.

"I still think it's too much like that Farm Family of the Year thing. Too much pride in it."

"You mean too much pride in speaking, or in not speaking?"

Well, she hadn't meant for it to come out quite like that, but she couldn't take it back. Bob downed the rest of the milk before he responded.

"Don't think I want to get into that discussion again at the moment, if you don't mind. I'm too tired, and besides that, I have no idea how Pete thinks he has enough time to go tripping up to Harding for errands, whatever that means. Maybe he forgot how much work we have to do."

"I'm sure he has his reasons."

"It's not my worry, except that it makes a lot more work for me. But never mind. I just need to get to bed. Maybe we can talk about this speaking thing again tomorrow."

Sure, and Bob would stumble into the kitchen the same way tomorrow night, exhausted from his field work. Wasn't he supposed to be scaling back on work, taking it easy? He rested his head in his hands, rubbing his eyes. The poor man did look worn out, and she didn't blame him for that.

"Sure, honey," she replied. "We can talk about it again tomorrow."

Chapter Fifteen

Pete scanned the sidewalk ahead of him and ducked into a nearby doorway, mostly out of sight of the Wednesday morning traffic on Harding's Main Street. Jiffy Dry-Kleen had not yet opened, but at five minutes to nine neither had many of the other businesses. He looked at his watch, just to be sure.

How long could this take? A couple of minutes to find something he could afford, and then a couple of minutes to get back to the truck and hurry back to Heather Creek Farm.

He figured he should be able to slip in and out of the jewelry store here without anyone he knew seeing him. This was Harding, after all, not Bedford. He could probably count on one hand the number of people he knew here. So naturally as he reached for the door handle of Harding Jewelers he heard his name called out.

"Peter Stevenson!"

Who called him Peter? He turned to see a small woman with sensible shoes, a knee-length skirt, and a bob of white hair hurrying his direction.

"Mrs. Litchfield." Pete sighed and tried to look more relaxed than he felt. "I haven't seen you in a couple of years. How are you?"

"Quite well, considering. You know I always enjoy running into my former students." She walked up next to him and sized him up as if he were standing for inspection. "You never did go on to college, did you?"

Pete smiled. What else could he do?

"I've been working on my family's farm, you know, Heather Creek. How is—"

"You had the potential to do well, Peter, if you had simply applied yourself more in your studies."

"Yes, ma'am. I—"

"But here you are, shopping at the local jeweler, so I assume your farm at least must be doing reasonably well."

"Oh, that?" Pete backed away from the door. "I'm, uh . . ."

This time she didn't interrupt, just kept her dark eyes on him the way she always had when he'd tried to sneak a Superman comic book in behind the volume of poetry they were supposed to be reading in freshman English.

"Actually, Mrs. Litchfield, the farm is doing great, but—"

"Your parents are well, I assume."

She straightened the shoulder strap of her large canvas purse. "Please be certain to greet them for me—and Miss Simons, as well."

"Miss Simons. Yeah, I mean, yes, sure. I will, thank you."

She obviously still kept up with all the news from Bedford, including how her former students were doing, whom they were dating, and what they'd had for breakfast.

How did she know? He wondered as he made his way down the sidewalk, watching Mrs. Litchfield out of the corner of his eye until she disappeared into a shop at the end of the block.

As soon as he was sure she wasn't coming right back out he made a quick about-face and returned to the jeweler. Bells hanging from the door jingled when he stepped inside, and a clerk standing behind a glass counter looked up with a smile.

"Good morning," the clerk greeted him. She could have been his mother's age or a couple of years younger. The best part was that he had never seen the woman before, and she would likewise have no idea who he was. "May I help you with anything?"

Pete looked around the small shop. The U-shaped showcase lined three walls. The shelves inside the case held bright displays of rings, bracelets, necklaces, and plenty of other expensive-looking jewelry.

He took a breath and pointed to a case of rings.

"Actually, yeah. I may be looking for a ring."

He wasn't fooling the woman behind the counter for a second; she looked as if she had to deal with stuttering farm boys every day. Without missing a beat, she moved to open one of the cases from behind.

"For a young lady, perhaps?"

"Right. You have, uh, engagement rings here?"

"Quite a few. Let me show you."

So far, so good. He rubbed the palms of his hands on his jeans and wondered why a little place like this had the heat cranked up so high. The saleslady didn't look warm though. She just smiled and pulled out a black velvet tray holding a collection of gold and silver bands with sparkling diamonds. Pete had never seen so many rings up close before. Ten minutes later he felt more confused than when he'd stepped in the door.

"So this is a three-stone, and this is platinum." Pete scratched his head and looked at yet another one. His eyes felt as if they were crossing. "And this one is the solitaire."

The clerk nodded patiently. She really did remind him of his mom.

"The one you're looking at is eighteen-carat white gold with the knife edge."

"And this one is the yellow gold."

"Correct. If she likes the classic look."

How did he know what she liked? As if they'd had deep conversations about jewelry styles.

"She's pretty classic. But..." He pointed to the little price tag. "You said that price doesn't include the diamond?"

"Not that one. On many of these we separate out the numbers so you can put them together any way you'd like. See, I'll show you how it works. It's not so hard."

"Too many choices." Pete shook his head and checked his watch. Twenty more minutes had passed. His dad would be wondering by now, for sure. "I had no idea it would be so complicated. And then there's the carats."

"I know it can seem a little overwhelming at first. But here, this is a very nice setting, just like the one you looked at."

This time she held up a solitaire with a clear, sparkling diamond, a little smaller than the others, but still nice. He glanced at the price tag and caught his breath yet again. Thank goodness he had put away that money he had gotten from the country–music video shoot back in the summer.

"I think she'd like this one." The salesclerk let him hold it up to the light. "It's very nice quality."

"Looks good to me."

He paused. This would have been a whole lot easier if they'd been talking horsepower instead of carats, or if this purchase came with a shop manual and was painted green. But if he was going to do this, he was just going to have to decide, and that would be that. By this time, his throat was feeling dry.

"Okay." He nodded. "This one."

Pete wasn't sure if the clerk would be getting a nice little commission on this sale, but she beamed as if she would.

"Excellent choice. We'll put this in a nice ring box for you. She's a very fortunate girl, you know."

"I guess I hadn't ever thought of it that way."

The clerk rang up his sale and gave him the information he needed about having the ring sized.

"And here, I have something else for you." She slipped a booklet into the small bag with HARDING JEWELERS, SINCE 1932 printed on the side.

"*Fifty Ways to Say, 'Will You Marry Me?'*" He glanced at the cover. "Guess that might come in handy. 'Course, all I need is one way that works."

"I'm sure you won't have any trouble," she told him, and that seemed like a nice thing to say, even if she really couldn't know one way or the other whether he was going to have troubles or not. Because by this time reality was starting to settle in, and his heart was racing as he accepted the small bag with the ring and the proposal how-to manual that he would probably need very much, thank you.

Did they offer refunds in case . . . ? No, he didn't even want to ask. Still, he hesitated, thinking again of Mrs. Litchfield on the street.

"Actually," he said, replacing his wallet in his back pocket. "You don't have any other bags, do you? Like just a plain bag?"

"I understand. Of course." The clerk quickly drew out a larger, unmarked bag and placed his purchase inside, book and all. "Our return policy is in there with the receipt as well. Not that you'll need it, of course, but we're required to tell you that."

"Oh." He stopped at the thought. The return policy. Anyway, he thanked her as he made his escape. Only problem was, he nearly ran straight into Mrs. Litchfield all over again as he was stepping back outside into the brisk autumn morning. How had he not seen her through the windows? Well, she had obviously seen him. He stepped aside to let her by, and she looked up at him with a hint of that smile that had appeared, when she mentioned Dana.

"Well, hello once again," she told him with mock surprise. "That's twice in one day. I was just coming in to have the battery on my watch replaced."

Pete wanted to say that she was probably coming in to pump the clerk for the latest details. But if she did, she did. He couldn't stop her.

"Well, you have a nice day, Mrs. Litchfield. See you again sometime."

Pete smiled politely as he held the door open with one hand and hid the bag behind his back with the other. As soon as he could, he stepped outside while Mrs. Litchfield leaned her head slightly for a better view of his prize. He made sure she didn't get it, however, as he kept walking toward his truck faster and faster. By the time he reached the curb he was nearly running like a little boy.

Once inside he slammed the door, caught his breath, and carefully set his purchase on the seat beside him. His hands were still sweating as he scanned the little book to see what advice it held.

"Let's see," he read. "Number one, hire a plane with an advertising banner that reads, 'Will you marry me, (insert name here)?'"

He thought about that one for a moment before laughing. Maybe a crop duster, but no. *Not my style.*

"Number two, order oysters at a restaurant and have the ring hidden in one of the shells."

Yeah, and where are we going to find oysters in Bedford? He was starting to get the feeling this book wasn't going to be much help after all.

"Number three, send a singing telegram."

Oh, come on. This was going from silly to worse. He tossed the book aside and started Lazarus up with a roar. He would have to read the rest of the book later, or else find his own way of proposing.

What am I doing? he asked himself. *And how in the world am I going to pull this off?*

And then he remembered what his dad had told him about life being too short to be messing around. That's what he was doing. Following Dad's advice for once. He looked down again at the plain brown bag, wondering if perhaps he should buckle it in. Given how much it cost, maybe that wasn't such a bad idea.

So maybe he wasn't sure what he was doing all the time. Maybe he didn't have a clue about this proposal business, or how it was going to happen. Maybe he didn't know if Dana would even say yes, assuming he could get up enough nerve to ask her.

One thing he could say for sure: This definitely was not messing around.

PETE DIDN'T NOTICE the unfamiliar truck parked next to the barn until he'd almost pulled up to the house. But even at a distance he could tell from Bob's body language that he wasn't in friendly mode.

Bob stood with his arms crossed, leaning away from the other fellow . . . and that would be Justin from TurboGen. Poor kid. Standing next to the open door of his own truck, he held a binder in his hand and seemed to be trying to show off a brochure.

But Bob obviously wasn't buying it. So Pete hurried to park his own truck and hopped out to try to smooth over the exchange.

"Hey, glad you stopped by!" Pete put on his cheery voice and smiled as best he could. He left the ring back on the seat of his truck for now. "I see you met Dad?"

"Er, yes." The young sales rep lowered his binder and looked over at Pete with obvious relief. "Your father and I were just chatting. He said you'd probably be back any minute."

"Well, here I am. What do we need to get started?"

"I need to set up some equipment in order to start taking some measurements."

"I'll let you guys figure things out." Bob interrupted and started to turn back to the barn where he'd parked his tractor. "Nice meeting you, er, Jason."

"That's Justin, Dad." Pete corrected him. But Bob only waved his hand without turning around. That was Dad for you.

"Sorry." Pete lowered his voice and tried to stay positive. "It just takes him a little more time to adjust to new ideas, you know?"

"Totally understandable," Justin said. "But I'm glad you decided to go ahead with the evaluation. I think there's a lot of potential around here. If you could just sign this paper giving us permission to set up on your property, I can get the ball rolling."

Pete accepted the paper with a nod.

"So what's next?" he asked.

The salesman pulled a little electronic organizer from his pocket and consulted the screen.

"I'm going to set up my measuring equipment on the hill there, if that's okay with you. Be back Friday . . . no, Saturday, to check it out and get more data. We'll go from there. I mean, if your dad's on board."

"Sure." Pete frowned. He didn't add, but Justin probably understood, that might be a very large *if*.

Chapter Sixteen

"What are you writing, Grandma?"

Christopher's question startled Charlotte, though it wouldn't have if she had been listening for the kids coming down the stairs for breakfast Thursday morning. She quickly shut her notebook, got up from the kitchen table, and returned to the oatmeal she'd been stirring on the stove.

"Nothing you'd be interested in." She ruffled Christopher's half-dry hair when he came up to inspect her progress. "Just a few thoughts."

Well, that was sufficiently vague. "A few thoughts" could be anything from a diary to the great American novel, though in this case it was most certainly neither.

"Kind of like what Ms. Luka makes us write in our notebooks every day, huh?"

"I don't know, Christopher. What does she make you write?"

"This week she wanted us to do something that ties into our science lesson. So I'm writing a story about a weatherman who invents a tornado-catching machine."

Christopher looked up at her as he deftly dipped a finger in the open package of brown sugar next to the stove. She let him think she hadn't seen.

"Well, that sounds like a much more exciting story than what I'm writing, dear. God has given you a very creative mind. Now, why don't you call the other kids and we'll have some breakfast."

As usual this month, she hadn't seen the men at all today, and might not again until well after dinner. She wasn't sure how they kept up with such long hours. Bob rose well before sunrise and stayed out in the fields until well after dark. He was probably starving out there. And the way things looked outside right then, with a slate overcast blotting out the sunrise, they could probably use a nice, steaming bowl of oatmeal. When Emily made it down the stairs a minute later, she took one look out the window and shivered.

"Looks like it's going to rain," she said.

"That's silly," replied Christopher. "There's only a 40 percent chance of showers today, with the barometer at forty-nine—"

"Never mind." Emily plopped down on a kitchen chair and absently blew the steam from her bowl as she stared out the window at the gray. "There's a 100 percent chance that I just don't feel like going to school today."

"Emily!" Charlotte brought toast and butter to the table. "What would make you say something like that?"

"Oh, that wedding dress project. It's just kind of, I don't know. Dragging, I guess."

"You spend enough time online." Sam joined them and

dumped more brown sugar on his oatmeal before dousing it with milk.

"Easy with that," Charlotte warned him. "It's already sweet enough. And Emily, I wish I could help you more, but you know how I am with that stuff."

Emily didn't answer and just nibbled on a plain piece of toast as if she had all the time in the world. This morning, however, Charlotte found herself eager to see the kids finally leave for school. Even before Sam's car had turned onto the main road twenty minutes later she had hurriedly rinsed off the breakfast dishes, and then scribbled a note for Bob in case he came back in before she returned from town.

"Gone to the rest home to check on Greta," she wrote. "Back after lunch."

Almost as an afterthought she tucked her notebook into her purse before she stepped out the back door. Maybe Greta would have some ideas.

"YOU DON'T NEED to feel strange about it."

Greta Harbinger seemed to understand what Charlotte was telling her as they sat in their usual chairs—Charlotte at the foot of the bed, near the window, and Greta next to her husband. Bud, as usual, had his eyes closed and rested his chin on his chest. He could still snore loudly enough to wake everyone else in the Bedford Gardens Convalescent Center.

"Well, yes, I know," replied Charlotte. "I don't mean *strange*, exactly. I just wish Bob and I could be doing this seminar together. As it is, I'm doing all the preparing, and he doesn't seem to want to talk about it."

"But he's agreed to speak to the group?"

"That's the thing. He said he didn't want to, but I kept pressing the issue, and we sort of left it unresolved."

"So he's reluctant to speak in public about matters that seem personal. You blame him for that?"

"No, no. But I suppose I never looked at it that way."

"From his perspective, you mean."

"Right. From . . . his perspective."

Charlotte wasn't sure how the conversation had taken this turn. But Greta's gnarled hands never stopped moving as she worked on a counted cross-stitch project. Though Charlotte couldn't make it out entirely, she would not have been surprised if Greta finished the cross-stitch before they were done with the talking. What else could Charlotte say to explain her side of the impasse?

"I suppose I just always thought he was coming up with excuses for not being willing to step out and try something new."

"That sounds a bit harsh, dear. Do you think he sees it that way?"

"No," Charlotte admitted. "Probably not."

"So how do you think he sees it?"

Charlotte had to think about that one for a moment.

"He said something about not wanting to appear prideful. He's always very sensitive about that."

She broke off the story before it began, not wanting to say too much. But when Greta spoke again, Charlotte knew she had come to the right place.

"Everyone has their reasons for wanting to do something like this, or not. But the way I see it, what else can you do but pray?"

Charlotte nodded and sighed. Greta didn't have any magic answers, just a sympathetic ear and a bit of wise counsel.

"Perhaps you'd like to read me what you've written so far?" Greta nodded at Charlotte's notebook.

"Oh, no." Charlotte gulped as she clutched the book. "There's really nothing here worth passing along. In fact, I'd be embarrassed."

"But you took the time to write it down. I'm sure there's something good there."

By this time Charlotte was certain there most definitely was not. She peeked down at her scribbled notes from this morning, and the lifeless outline reminded her of a report she might have given back in her school days, with topics numbered one through five: mutual respect, open communication, consideration for each other's feelings, and so on. Very correct, and yet very predictable. She could have easily crumpled the notes up on the spot.

"Actually . . ." She looked up hopefully. "I was hoping perhaps you could tell me what you would say. What would you say if you had to tell a room full of young couples how to have a lasting marriage?"

"That's a big topic, isn't it?" Greta smiled and looked over at her sleeping husband. Charlotte took notes as quickly as she could as Greta spoke softly of her married years and what they had meant to her. She told of the harder times—when they had lost a baby, and how supportive Bud had been. She told of the lean years, the times when Bud's business didn't do as well and they had to eat canned beans for dinner, but how they had made a pact never to argue about money. And when she told of their golden anniversary, when Bud had surprised her with a Caribbean cruise, her eyes danced.

"I don't think he really enjoyed the cruise all that much," she said. "He was seasick the first several days. But he loved making me happy, and he loved surprising me. He was always surprising me, buying me gifts for no reason, or making me laugh."

Charlotte wrote down everything she could, even though she would have rather put down her pen to just listen to the life stories.

"I imagine I'm not the first person to ask you about the secret to your long marriage." Charlotte tried not to sound overly inquisitive, but her question apparently made Greta chuckle.

"It's no secret, but yes, I've been asked that question a number of times. My answer, *our* answer, has always been the same."

She looked to her husband and stroked his knee as he raised his head.

"Honey," she told him, "Charlotte wants to know how we've been married so long. What's our secret?"

Well, that took several moments to register with Bud, as did most things. She raised her voice and took his left hand in hers, the one with his wedding band.

"How have we been—"

"The dog," he interrupted her, looking down at his ring. "Did you feed the dog?"

"The dog's fine," she told him, unfazed. "We've been married sixty-two years. You remember?"

He looked back at her as if considering the question, and then furrowed his brow in concentration. But he did not answer.

Did any part of him still remember? Charlotte could not be sure as he turned his attention to the lively red cardinal scratching at the bird feeder outside their window. He started humming a song that sounded a lot like a fractured Jimmy Dorsey tune, and the awkward exchange made Charlotte want to rewind the past few minutes.

"I'm sorry." She picked up her notebook. "Perhaps I shouldn't have bothered you."

But Greta would have none of it.

"Dear, you really shouldn't say that. You're never a bother. In fact, I think Bud enjoys your visits almost as much as I do. Don't you, Bud?"

By this time Bud was fully engrossed in watching the bird. But once more, that didn't appear to disturb Greta in the least. In fact, nothing seemed to upset the woman, and she turned to look Charlotte in the eye.

"I know your Bob is a good provider, just like my Bud. Bud always did so much for me when he was still able. In fact, just a couple of years ago, I caught him trying to get up on the roof of our little house. He said he didn't want the snow to fall on me, or the roof to cave in. I was scared to death he might fall, you know?"

Charlotte couldn't help but smile at the story. That sounded very much like Bob. Greta went on.

"You asked how we've been married this long, but I think you already know the answer, dear. We've remembered our vows to each other, just as you have. We've looked for the best in each other. And we've kept our faith. I think you've found that in your husband, as well."

Well, this hadn't quite turned out the way Charlotte expected. She gathered up her purse to stand, but Greta still wasn't done.

"And here, I want you to have this. It's not framed, but perhaps your Bob knows how to do that sort of thing better than I would. He sounds handy."

With all her writing, Charlotte hadn't noticed that Greta had finished the cross-stitch project, and she now held it out to her. Charlotte caught her breath at the intricate work and ran her fingertips across the lovely red lettering and the heart border on a dappled off-white linen.

"Love does not consist in gazing at each other," she read, "but in looking outward together in the same direction."

And now Charlotte didn't quite know what to say, except a jumbled mixture of "I couldn't" and "you shouldn't." None of it made any sense.

"Of course you must," Greta answered with a shy smile, leaving her work in Charlotte's hands as she folded up her thread and scissors and placed them in her workbasket. "And why shouldn't I? It's something to fill the time, to help me feel just a tiny bit useful."

As they stood Charlotte thanked Greta with a hug, fearing she might leave the home once again with tears in her eyes.

"More than a tiny bit useful," Charlotte replied, her voice choking. "You have no idea."

"Good." That seemed to satisfy Greta. "Now I don't know if that gives you any more to say at the seminar. But

I'm certain everything is going to work out with your husband, one way or the other. I'm praying for you two."

Charlotte wished she could say the same thing, and with just as much certainty. But all she could do was clutch her prize as she left, wondering how she could begin to be as good a role model as Greta Harbinger.

Chapter Seventeen

Emily tapped her pen on the edge of the table in the computer lab, waiting for the flatbed scanner to do its thing. She checked the clock on the wall. Four fifteen.

This was taking forever. It seemed as if this scanner were older than she was. In fact, all this Thursday afternoon she'd only been able to scan three photos, even though she and Ashley had been working here for more than an hour after school. Pretty soon Eddie the janitor would be kicking them out, and she wasn't near done.

"Come on, machine," she mumbled as the scanner hummed and fussed some more. She lifted the hinged cover a little too soon and had to blink at the halo of bright green light around Grandma's old photo, which was lying facedown on the glass.

"Whoops!" Snapping the cover back down, she hoped the scan of Grandma in her fancy wedding dress wasn't ruined. It had to look perfect for her report on "Wedding Dress Styles, 1850 to the Present."

Pretty good title, she thought. Sounded like an award-winning documentary, right? Their teacher, Mrs. Johnston, was going to like it for sure—if she ever got these scans finished.

"How's it going over there, Em?" Ashley called from the workstation on the other side of the room, where she was working on her own report detailing the life of Princess Diana. "You done yet?"

Like Emily, Ashley had been trying to scan a ton of photos, which she would then place in between the written parts of her report using PowerPoint. It made for more work up front, but she didn't think anyone else in their computer science class would have as cool-looking reports as they would.

"Last one for now," she told Ashley, "if it turns out."

She held her breath but finally a clear black-and-white image of Grandma in her dress popped up on the screen. Yes! Maybe it had come out a little darker than Emily would have liked, but she could fix that. So she zoomed in on Grandma standing on the church steps, trimmed most of the background, and prepared to save the photo to her collection. Meanwhile Ashley came up from behind and looked over Emily's shoulder.

"You're kidding, right?" Ashley giggled. "Show me how you did that."

"Did what?" Emily wasn't sure what her friend was saying. "You've been doing the same thing with your photos."

"No, I mean, like you cut and pasted your face into the old photo, right? That's hilarious! You should show that to my mom: Emily in a wedding dress!"

"That's not my face, silly. That's . . ."

But as Emily looked a little more closely at the photo,

she realized what Ashley was talking about, and what she had sort of noticed the first time she saw the photo. Kind of like one of those puzzles where you can't see the hidden picture at first, but then it clicks in your mind and you can't miss it. Well, it had just clicked. And while it definitely was Grandma in the photo, now Emily couldn't help seeing her own eyes there too, as if she were looking in a mirror. The shape of the face was a lot like her own too. Maybe even the tight-lipped little smile.

"I guess it does kind of look like me," she admitted. "But it really is Grandma. I didn't do anything to the photo except crop it."

"For real? That's spooky." Ashley shook her head. "I was, like, totally sure that was you. Did you know you guys looked so much alike?"

"Not until you mentioned it. I always thought I kind of looked like my mom. But I guess the picture was taken when Grandma was only a couple years older than we are now."

"Yeah. People used to get married pretty young, huh?"

"That's the scary part, if you ask me."

"Oh, I don't know. One of my cousins got married when she was eighteen."

Emily rolled her eyes at the thought.

"Spare me, please. I can't even imagine."

By this time Ashley was looking out the window as a couple of seniors jogged by in their cross-country outfits. One of them smiled and waved at her, and her cheeks flushed as she waved back. Oh, brother. No telling what was on that girl's mind.

Emily didn't have time to wonder though. She finished trimming and touching up the photo before saving it once more and shutting down for the day. And just in time too.

"You girls still in here?" Eddie the janitor poked his balding head into the computer lab. His eyes looked double-size behind big glasses that seemed as if they might have been salvaged from somewhere, as if he had found them in the trash or on the floor. "'Cause I'm locking up, and—"

"We're done." Ashley came to attention, grabbed her books off the nearby table, and turned to Emily. "Just leaving. Right, Emily?"

Well, they were, almost. Emily hurried to finish up and put her things in her backpack.

"Let's go, Emily!" Ashley held the door open. By now Ashley's mom would be waiting for them in her dark blue minivan out in front of the school.

Good timing. Mrs. Givens honked and waved at the girls as they pushed out the front door and scurried to the van.

"Can Emily eat dinner with us?" asked Ashley, even before she had asked Emily. Well, Emily thought that would be okay, as long as it was okay with Ashley's mom. And Grandma.

"You just give your grandmother a call as soon as we get home." Ashley's mom said as she placed the car into gear and pulled away from the school.

Several minutes later at Ashley's house, Emily did just that, although Grandma paused and her voice sounded a little strained over the phone when she said, "Well, all right."

"I'll do my chores when I get home," Emily promised, and Grandma replied that yes, she was sure she would.

But chores were the last thing on Emily's mind as she looked at the take-home smorgasbord of goodies from Mel's Place. They didn't eat dinners like this at home.

"Sorry it's leftover night from the restaurant," said Mrs. Givens as they sat down at the table. "I grabbed what I could as I was leaving. Good thing I brought a few extras."

"Well, I'm glad you could make it home tonight," said Ashley's dad, sniffing at the chicken and addressing Melody. "Most Thursdays we aren't so lucky."

"It was slow today." Mrs. Givens smiled. "And Ginny needed the hours, so I was able to escape. It's nice Emily could be here with us too."

Emily and Ashley sat on one side of the table, Mr. and Mrs. Givens on either end, and Ashley's older brother, Brett, on the other side. When Mr. Givens nodded, they reached out and grasped hands. Though Emily wasn't used to this kind of prayer, she was quick enough to follow along. Fortunately Mrs. Givens was on her right, and Ashley on her left.

"Jesus, you are so good to us," began Mr. Givens, his voice loud and clear. This wasn't the way Grandpa prayed, but it was kind of nice. "This is even more than we need, but we're grateful to you. And not just for the food, but for each one here. For bringing Emily to share it with us. We praise you, in the precious name of the Savior, amen!"

Each of the others echoed his amen, and Emily felt her hands being squeezed. She kind of liked how they prayed here. Ashley's dad looked over at her and waved his hand across the table.

"And the good news is, Emily, the guest gets to choose whatever she likes."

"Oh! Well, how do I choose?" Emily looked over the steaming trays of chicken wings, spaghetti with meatballs, elbow macaroni with white sauce, scalloped potatoes, and a green-bean dish smothered in a blend of cream of onion soup and crumbles. She had to admit it smelled awfully good. So she took a little bit of everything, avoiding the meatballs and the wings, and she waited for the others to pass everything around. Nobody bugged her about not eating meat, and Brett didn't get any heat for not taking vegetables. This, thought Emily, was a little closer to life as it should be.

"Ashley tells me you're doing your project on wedding dresses," said Mrs. Givens, ladling up some pasta for herself. "I should tell you about mine."

"Actually," added Ashley, "you should use some of Mom's wedding photos, so you could have, like, a couple of generations. Right, Mom?"

That was okay with Emily if it was okay with Mrs. Givens, who actually had a very cool story, since her dress had originally been featured in a fashion magazine of some sort—a model had worn it first. Then it was going to be auctioned off for charity.

"So how did you get it?" Emily wanted to know.

"Ah, that's the fun part," replied Mrs. Givens, helping herself to a chicken wing. "See, one of my girlfriends from high school, her mom had a friend of a friend in New York with some kind of connection . . ."

By this time Brett's eyes were glazing over at the story—

maybe he'd heard it before—but that was okay. The girls talked dresses all through dinner, and then after dinner, while Mr. Givens did the dishes, Mrs. Givens pulled down a photo album from the top shelf of a hall closet to show Emily a few pictures.

"It's beautiful!" said Emily. The style wasn't exactly what most girls would wear these days, but Mrs. Givens hadn't been kidding about the dress. Without Emily even asking, she let her borrow the photo for her PowerPoint presentation, along with a yellowed clipping from the *Bedford Leader* with the write-up about the dress.

"Wow," said Emily. "This is definitely cool."

Everybody, it seemed, had a cool story to tell about their wedding dress. But Ashley sighed as they plopped down on her bed a little later.

"And I had to choose something totally boring for my report," she said.

"Totally boring? Since when is Princess Diana boring?" Emily picked a magazine off Ashley's nightstand to prove her point. "See? Look at this dress she's wearing. It's gorgeous!"

The conversation went on like that for a while, from wedding dresses and princesses to boys and who was cute. They purposely avoided the topic of school for as long as they could, until the phone rang somewhere out in the house. A moment later Ashley's mom knocked on the door.

"Girls?" she asked. "Do you realize what time it is?"

As a matter of fact... Emily glanced at Ashley's bedside alarm clock for the first time since they'd retreated to the room and almost choked.

"Is that clock right?" she gasped as Ashley turned to see and her mom stepped into the room. "We just sat down on the bed for a minute."

As it turned out, a bit more than a minute had passed. Funny how they'd lost track.

"I am so sorry, Emily." Mrs. Givens acted as if it were her fault that it was almost nine. "You two were so quiet in here that I totally forgot you were here. Your grandma just called."

"Did she sound upset?"

"Well, she *was* wondering." Ashley's mom herded them out into the hallway, grabbed her car keys off a hook by the kitchen door, and led the way back out to the van. "I told her we're on our way."

Just minutes later they were flying down Heather Creek Road in the direction of home.

"Mom!" Ashley braced herself against the dashboard as if for impact. "You always tell Dad to slow down."

"Goodness, you're right. Better to get there in one piece, isn't it?"

Soon enough they pulled into the gravel driveway where Emily said her thanks to Mrs. Givens for dinner and everything. When she felt her backpack, though, she had to wonder. A little lighter, maybe? She took a quick peek inside and paused.

"Uh-oh," she whispered.

"You just tell your grandmother it was all my fault," Ashley's mom told her as they pulled up to the back door.

"No, that's not it." Emily felt around her pack one more time to be sure. "I think I left my photos somewhere. The ones from Grandma?"

"Probably back in my bedroom," Ashley assured her. "I'll bring them to school tomorrow."

Emily thanked her, but it still bugged her that she couldn't remember the last time she'd had her hands on those photos. If she lost them, well, she was toast—or worse.

Speaking of which, she probably still had some explaining to do when she got inside. What about the chores she had promised to do when she got home? She wondered if there might be a way to slip in the back door without being noticed, but decided against it when the back porch light snapped on.

"Here, let me talk to your grandma again for a moment," said Mrs. Givens, slipping out from behind the wheel. That would be okay with Emily. Better than having to explain it all by herself, for sure. With a wave to Ashley, she stepped out into the cool October night.

For a moment she stood in the dark shadow behind the van, her breath fogging around her like clouds in the starry sky. Another pale light flickered across the gravel courtyard, and she looked up to see Uncle Pete silhouetted in his little second-story window.

He wasn't looking out at the stars or the van, though, but pacing and waving his hands, as if he were making some kind of speech or arguing with someone on the phone. Only he wasn't holding any phone, as far as she could tell.

What in the world?

Chapter Eighteen

"No, no, no . . ."

Pete was just about ready to toss the stupid little book into the trash where it belonged, when he finally noticed the headlights below and pulled back from the window.

Shoot! Did they see me?

He didn't think so. Just in case, though, he retreated to the bedroom, wondering who would be visiting his folks' house at this time of night. The minivan looked like the one Melody Givens drove, but he couldn't be sure. Melody wouldn't have any reason to stop by the house at . . . what was it, almost nine-thirty?

Never mind. Right now he had more important issues to deal with. He gripped the little book and turned the page.

"Way to Propose, Number Twenty-two," he read, the heat in his face rising as he paced at the foot of his bed. This one would be just as lame as all the others. "Take out a full-page ad in your local newspaper, and . . . no."

He sighed and turned the page again. No way in the world would he embarrass Dana or himself that way. Not a chance. He looked over at the ring box sitting on his dresser. As it turned out, buying the ring—hard as that had been—was by far the easiest part of this assignment.

"There's got to be a better way," he told himself out loud. "Not skywriting, not full-page ads, not dragging her out to the middle of the basketball court at halftime, not a bunch of kids wearing lettered T-shirts spelling out 'Will you marry me?' None of that."

He paced as he leafed through the rest of the book, and when he turned to the last page he really did hurl the booklet across the room, sending it with a satisfying plunk into the middle of his little trash basket.

"Two points."

But still he had no plan. What was he supposed to do, just stop by the teachers' lounge at lunchtime, the way he always did, and hold out the ring to her? That would be just as bad as skywriting or any one of the other forty-nine dopey suggestions he'd read.

One way or another, though, he knew he had to come up with something good. Something classy. Because she would be telling the story to friends and strangers, maybe for the rest of her life.

If he were that lucky, she would. And if he were lucky, she would have something worth telling. But at the moment the tension between what he thought he really wanted to do and the frightening reality of actually pulling it off made his temples throb and his stomach ache.

"Lord, what am I supposed to do, now?" he prayed as he place-kicked a paper sack on the floor. The receipt for the ring fluttered out at his feet along with another slip of paper. What? He stooped to pick up what the clerk had slipped in with his purchase, along with the ring and the book.

The Harding Jewelers Easy Return Policy. He hoped that was not his answer from God.

PETE FINGERED THE CRUMPLED return policy in his jeans pocket as he stood outside the door of the Bedford High teachers' lounge at lunch the next day. Why hadn't he just thrown the silly thing away already? He couldn't really answer his own question. But Jenny Thomas noticed him as she swept by in the crowd of students passing by.

"Hey, Petey. Looking for someone to have lunch with?" Jenny had attended Bedford High a year or two behind Pete, and it seemed her smile was a little too bright today.

"Right. You seen Dana?"

Her face fell as she pointed at the door. But Pete didn't need directions; he already knew where to look. Still he nodded his thanks and pushed his way inside, away from the commotion of the hallway. How did Dana put up with all the noise day after day? He was just glad it was her and not him. A person could only take so much.

Here in the teachers' lounge four or five teachers talked quietly at round tables, huddled over their lunches of skinny sandwiches and carrot sticks. Harry Edlesheim smiled and waved from where he stood in front of the microwave, heating what smelled like leftover lasagna.

No one else took much note of Pete though. By now he'd become a regular in the staff room, visiting several times a week. Mrs. Boyd at the reception desk didn't even make him wear a visitor's name tag anymore, as she'd done the first couple of times.

Funny, though, how the uneasy feeling in the pit of his stomach never left him. He glanced at his stained jeans and realized maybe he was a little underdressed. Everyone in the lounge wore neat skirts and blouses or pressed slacks—what, for Pete would be Sunday clothes. Even Harry, digging into his hot lasagna, wore brown cords, an off-white shirt, and a crooked green tie.

Not that Pete officially cared. Everyone knew where he came from. It just felt a little odd today. And it didn't help that Dana looked extra-nice in a navy suit coat—the kind that professional women would wear—along with an ivory blouse and tan slacks. She would have been at home in any office, and so would her principal, Chad Duncan. They huddled in the corner by the sink, obviously deep in discussion.

Dana apparently hadn't noticed Pete. Instead she nodded intently as Mr. Duncan explained something to her in a language Pete couldn't even faintly comprehend.

Somebody get me a translator, he thought, leaning against a file cabinet and waiting for the conversation to wind up. But as they continued in their animated chatter he felt himself buried in a fog of words like—"disaggregation of results," "cognitive complexity," and "equity-sensitive performance assessments." And Dana, there could be no doubt, was enjoying every minute of it.

"Mr. Stevenson." Harry Edlesheim still called Pete "Mister," for reasons unknown. He approached with a mouthful of lasagna. "How's the harvest coming?"

"Oh yeah." Pete straightened up. "The harvest. Well, we're

anticipating exceptional crop yields this season with the, er, application of highly advanced techniques."

Best he could do. But Harry just kind of wrinkled up his nose at him, so Pete gave it another shot.

"Doin' good, Harry."

That brought a puzzled smile of recognition to Harry's face as he juggled his lunch with a can of Coke ... and Dana finally noticed.

"Pete! I didn't see you come in." She smiled at him, and then looked toward her principal, as if asking for permission to call a time-out. Principal Duncan folded up his notebook, slipped it into his jacket pocket, and nodded.

"Another time then." He excused himself and left the lunchroom.

"Got time to run to Mel's Place?" Pete asked Dana, but she frowned as she checked her watch.

"I'm sorry. I have some papers I need to grade, and I promised Mr. Duncan I'd help him with some, well, you wouldn't ..."

Her voice trailed off, and she looked around as if everyone were listening. But this time Pete didn't care.

"I wouldn't what?" He kept his voice down, in any case.

"Come on, Pete." She took his arm and guided him toward the door. "Walk with me back to my classroom."

That's when Pete remembered exactly why he'd dropped out of school early, despite the strenuous objections of his family. He hated the feeling of his teacher, Miss Ventura, grabbing his arm and marching him out of the room to the principal's office. He hated the feeling of being talked down to, like he wouldn't be able to understand. He hated the smell of the hallways and the jostle of getting to class on time, only four minutes between classes, and the unending "sit down and do your work."

He hated the straitjacket of school, the disapproving stares from teachers, the girls who always got A's on their papers because they sat in the front row and never got into trouble. He hated it all.

"Pete, what's wrong?" Dana looked at him strangely as she released his arm and they walked together toward her classroom. By this time the halls had mostly cleared out, which was a good thing, and he planted the heel of his boot squarely on the tile floor, leaving a scuff mark that Dana noticed with obvious disapproval. Maybe she sent students to the office for less.

"Look, I'm sorry I bothered you," he told her. "I thought Thursdays were a good time to see you, but I can tell you're busy today. I'll go."

The worst part was, she didn't try to stop him or talk him out of it. He left another scuff mark as he pivoted and headed for the nearest set of double doors. Didn't matter that they opened out to the alley in back of the cafeteria where dumpsters were parked. He just needed to make a quick exit.

"I'm sorry, Pete," she called after him. "Will you call me tonight?"

"Sure," he replied without turning. "Tonight."

He felt in his pocket to be sure the Harding Jewelers Easy Return Policy was still there, and for the first time he was a little relieved to have it with him.

What am I doing here? he asked himself, hurrying past the smell of spoiled french fries and around the parking lot to where his good-enough truck was parked next to a sensible green hybrid sedan that a schoolteacher would be proud to drive. For the first time he noticed just how much his truck stood out. Had he really not seen it this way before?

Who am I kidding?

No, he couldn't imagine Dana driving the truck to work if she had the misfortune to marry a farmer like him. Not that she would have to, or that he would ask her to. But the possibilities were beginning to crumble.

What's more, he couldn't imagine Dana getting horse manure on the nice black shoes she wore to class. Heck, she didn't even speak the same language as he did, and he sure wasn't going to embarrass himself trying to pretend he was someone he wasn't. He didn't belong here, and he felt the gap widen between his world and Dana's as never before.

What was I thinking?

By this time he couldn't even imagine how Dana would agree to live in a little apartment above a tractor shed, within sight of her in-laws, surrounded by the raw smell of fields and fertilizer and acres of dirt. She didn't deserve that kind of life, but he knew he couldn't offer her much more.

Why embarrass myself trying?

So he climbed into the truck and jammed the key into the ignition. The truck hesitated and clicked, and he pounded the steering wheel with his free left hand.

"Not now, you old—"

Lazarus must have heard him. The truck roared back to life, so Pete wasted no time grinding the gears and escaping the campus—just as he had when he was a teenager. The only difference was, this time, instead of a patch of rubber, he left behind a piece of his heart. And the worst part was, he had no idea how to retrieve it.

Chapter Nineteen

"What do you think's eating him, Britney?" Charlotte offered the horse another sugar cube as she watched her son from across the barn. First Pete pitched a bale of hay into the trailer behind his tractor, and then he knocked over a pile of buckets, sending wood scraps flying.

Without pausing to pick anything up, Pete hopped up into the seat and jammed it into gear with a grunt and a nasty grinding sound.

In a hurry? wondered Charlotte, scurrying over to help open the double doors that had swung shut. No telling where Bob had disappeared to that Friday afternoon. But for a moment it looked as if Pete would crash right through without stopping, until Charlotte waved her hands for him to stop.

"Whoa, take it easy, there!" She reached across to the door and swung it open wide as Pete revved the tractor. "No sense breaking down the door."

Pete probably didn't hear her over the roar of the engine, but nodded his thanks as he tried to scoot by. Charlotte, on the other hand, had to hop back so the tractor didn't run over her toes.

"Here," she told Pete, raising her voice and pointing, "let me get that other..."

Too late. The tractor's front tire had already nudged the other door, swinging it out while nearly popping the hinges in the process. At the same time one of the tractor wheel hubs caught on the first door, tearing through a handful of splinters. Once more Pete didn't seem to notice, but Charlotte winced at the sound.

"Pete!" This was too much. She yelled her son's name as loudly as she could: "PETE!"

Well, that stopped him—for the moment.

"What's up?" Pete yelled over the engine noise.

"That's what I want to know," Charlotte yelled back. "Here, would you please just idle down for a moment?"

That appeared to be the last thing Pete wanted to do, but he finally sagged his shoulders and complied as Charlotte stepped around to the front to keep him from driving off.

"Look, Pete." She took a deep breath. "You're banging around and about to tear the whole barn down. So if something's bothering you, maybe you should get it out in the open. You know, before you cause any more damage?"

"Sorry about that. I'm just trying to get my work done, okay?"

Charlotte held up her hands in surrender. If the boy wasn't going to talk, she certainly couldn't make him. Even so, there was no reason for all this foolishness.

"You sure that's all? You haven't said a word to anyone all day. All you've done is grunt. You've been throwing things around. And your eyes are so bloodshot, it looks like you didn't sleep all night. Did I leave anything out?"

"How about, I haven't eaten anything all week."

"What?"

"Just kidding, Mom. I've been eating. I do have my own kitchen, you know. There's just a lot of work to get done and only so many hours in a day."

"I know all about your work. We all have a lot of work. But I'm your mother, and I can tell something else is wrong."

Pete frowned, pulled down the brim of his dusty red cap, and crossed his arms. Perhaps Charlotte would not have called herself a body language expert, but she had a pretty good idea what Pete was trying to say. And this conversation was apparently over.

"All right then." Charlotte finally moved back from the tractor. No sense being run over. "I'm not trying to poke my nose where it's not welcome. I just know something's bothering you. And if you ever want to talk about it, I'm available. So is your father."

Pete closed his eyes for a moment, as if considering whether to share something. Then he shook his head.

"Look, Mom, I appreciate the concern, but—"

"It's about Dana, isn't it?"

Charlotte couldn't help blurting it out. But now Pete turned red in the face and didn't say anything. She waited as long as she could until he finally answered.

"It's not just about her, and it's for sure not her fault, Mom." Pete narrowed his eyes.

"Of course it's not. No one's saying that. I just want you two to work it out, whatever it is."

"Thanks. We will."

The tractor sputtered and almost died, just like their mother-to-son talk. Pete mumbled something about getting back to work as he revved up the tractor once again. Charlotte could only watch him drive away and out of sight around the corner of the barn.

Why doesn't he talk to his father about this sort of thing? she wondered. His father, however, was nowhere to be seen.

Over by the house, Toby was sitting in the middle of the gravel driveway, obviously waiting for the kids. Funny how that dog's sense of timing worked. In just a few minutes, she would bark at Sam's little car when he dropped Emily and Christopher off on his way to soccer practice. Unless the car broke down again, or Sam ran out of gas, or something else happened that Charlotte couldn't control.

Charlotte sighed as she retreated to the safety of her warm kitchen, where she could much better control the outcome of her life—or at least her cooking.

Why couldn't everywhere be like the kitchen?

EMILY RIFLED THROUGH HER LOCKER one more time, just to be sure. They had to be here somewhere!

"Come on, Emily," Ashley called out to her from the double doors at the end of the hallway. "Your brother's not going to wait for us much longer. He's going to be late to his soccer practice."

"Tell him I'll be right there. I just have to find those old photos."

"Right now?" Ashley stepped aside to let several kids pass through. "What's the big deal?"

"The big deal is that I promised my grandma I wouldn't lose them, and they're really important to her."

"You'll find them." Ashley headed outside. "I'll tell Sam to wait . . ."

Her voice faded as she joined the after-school parade to the parking lot, where Sam was waiting impatiently for them.

Emily made one more check of her locker, just to be sure they weren't there. She had even kept them in a special envelope, just so this kind of thing wouldn't happen. A lot of good that had done her.

"Not in the locker," she told herself, doing her best to retrace her steps. She wasn't coming up with anything useful. Where else could they be? "Oh, brother."

Emily kept her eyes glued to the floor of the hallway, just in case the envelope had slipped out of her backpack and been kicked into a dusty corner somewhere between her classes. Not likely. But theoretically it could have happened. Meanwhile she ran to the computer lab down the hall for one more look.

"Come on!" She rattled the doorknob and gave the bottom of the door a well-aimed kick. Where was Eddie the janitor when you needed him?

"Emily!" Ashley called one more time. "He's leaving!"

Emily sighed and gave the hallway one last look. She'd have to search again tomorrow—or make that Monday. If the old photos weren't at Ashley's, maybe they were home somewhere after all.

Maybe. She just couldn't remember, and that's what irked her the most.

"Coming!" she yelled back as she raced for the exit. Ashley was still waiting for her at the doors, but without her usually sunny expression.

"Take your time," she told Emily, a hand on her hip. "Sam and Christopher already left."

BOB WATCHED PETE ROAR BY on the tractor, looking as if a storm cloud was hovering over his head.

What's eating him? he wondered. Bob still needed to pick up a couple of sacks of feed that afternoon before the feed store closed. He felt for the keys in his pocket as he walked over to the pickup, avoiding a tennis ball tossed his way. Toby bounded past.

"Can I come, Grandpa?" asked Christopher. "I'm looking for trucks that match those tire tracks up by the you-know-what."

Bob shook his head and slammed the truck door after himself. "Not this time, pal. I'll be right back."

"I thought Grandma didn't want you driving, with your bad eyes."

"You tell your grandma I just need to get some chicken feed."

Well, maybe he did and maybe he didn't, but at the moment he just needed a good reason for getting away—and that was the best he could think of. Actually, though, a guy couldn't ever have enough chicken feed. Just like a guy could never have enough tools. So he hurried to start the engine and put the truck in reverse before Charlotte herself came outside to stop him. That left Christopher standing outside, tossing Toby's ball in one hand. Before anyone could ask more questions Bob was bumping down the driveway on his way to town.

And really, what was the problem? He made it to the Bedford Feed & Seed just fine and didn't hit anything along the way. He pulled up in front of the little metal-clad warehouse and parked. So there. Nothing to worry about. He could still drive as well as anyone. A little more squinting and straining, but oh well.

Once inside the feed store he took his time, waiting behind another customer, a woman who needed help choosing the right bridle and some dog food. As always, the Feed & Seed smelled like hay, cracked corn, and a hundred other dusty but pleasant blends of animal feed—for everything from draft horses and large farm animals to cats and dogs, pigeons and hamsters. If it flew, crawled, or lived in a barn, Ernie could sell you something to keep it well fed and healthy—as he had for almost as long as Bob could remember.

Once the woman with the bridle had exited with her purchase, the Feed & Seed owner leaned up against his counter behind the cash register and pushed the bill of his blue cap back over his mostly bald head.

"Them chickens of yours hungry again, Bob?"

"Starving." Bob played along with Ernie's banter. "By now I figure it'd be cheaper to buy our eggs at Herko's than to keep feeding 'em all the time."

"Which is why you're here."

"Well, somebody's got to keep you in business."

"You got that right. But hey, I heard you guys are going to set up one of those fancy new windmills on your place."

"You did, huh?" Bob raised his eyebrows.

"Hear it's a gravy deal. They put it up; you collect the checks. I'd have 'em put one on top of my house here in town, if they were interested. But good for you."

"Uh... yeah. Right."

Bob wasn't sure where Ernie got his facts. But so it went—the usual manly chitchat before getting down to the business of buying and selling—interrupted only by the jangle of the old wall phone next to the bulletin board with hand-written ads for everything from weaner pigs to bunnies and German shepherd pups.

"Feednseed." Ernie answered the same way he had for the past thirty years. He nodded a couple of times. "Sure thing, Charlotte. He's standing right here next to me. You want me to put him on the line?"

Bob hesitated a moment but took the receiver. He wasn't surprised at Charlotte's tone of voice either.

"Christopher told me you left in a hurry," she said. He could imagine the look on her face, and he pulled the phone cord with him around the corner. "I thought we agreed you'd let me drive for the next few days, until your surgery."

"I can see fine, and I didn't cause any accidents." He would change the subject as quickly as he could, and ignored her mention of the laser thing. "You need me to pick you up something here in town?"

Her sigh came through loud and clear.

"I just want you to be safe, that's all. And now Emily just called from school and said she needs a ride home. Ashley's mother can't leave the restaurant, and—"

"I'll pick her up."

"No! That's not what I meant at all. Sam was going to bring her home, but she was late and he had to go to soccer practice."

"I said I'll get her. We'll be home soon."

She sounded none too happy about that, but he hung up the phone and returned to his business. Ernie had his receipt ready, except the print was so tiny on the thing, a person couldn't be expected to see where he was supposed to sign.

"Forget your glasses, huh, Bob?" Ernie pointed out the blank line at the bottom so Bob could scribble his signature.

"Something like that. Thanks, Ernie."

"Yeah, you tell them chickens they can just keep eating all they want. I need to pay for my grandkids' college. And that windmill of yours is going to help too."

Bob wasn't sure about that, but just to prove a point he hefted a fifty-pound sack of chicken scratch over his shoulder and carried it out to the truck while Ernie followed with the second sack on a handcart. Some things a guy just had to do on his own, even if it nearly knocked him over in the process. And if he couldn't handle it, well, he'd cross that bridge when he came to it.

"There ya go." Ernie tossed the second sack in the back of the truck. Bob waved his thanks and headed off in the direction of the high school to pick up his granddaughter. Less than five minutes later Emily slid in next to him with her backpack and slammed the passenger door shut with a thud.

"So I get to ride in the truck today, huh?" When she smiled at him it was as if someone had turned the lights on for the first time all day. "Thought Grandma was going to pick me up."

"Sam's still at soccer practice; Grandma called me at the Feed & Seed so I'd pick you up on my way home."

"She did? I thought she wasn't letting you drive."

"How was school?" He ignored her question, and she hesitated only a moment before answering.

"Okay, I guess. It's Friday anyway, so that's good."

"Homework?" He placed the truck in gear.

"That project, still. The one with the dresses?"

Well, that didn't make a whole lot of sense, so Emily had to back up and explain about the presentation that she had to give. She talked about it as if he would know, and he wasn't about to give her reason to think otherwise. And he did know for a fact that kids these days were practically born with devices in their hands and knew how to make 'em do all kinds of things. She pulled a sheet of paper from her backpack.

"This is just a printout from a scan. It's not very good; the scanner at school is really junky. The real photo is . . ." She frowned in thought for a moment. "Well, it's somewhere. Anyway, you might recognize this dress. But don't look now, Grandpa."

Too late. He couldn't exactly focus on the road and Emily's printout at the same time, so he must have swerved just a little as they drove down Heather Creek Road.

"Watch out, Grandpa! There's a stop sign!"

He saw it plainly, and he had fully intended to stop. Just not quite as suddenly.

The good news was that no one else was around to see, so really there was no harm done. Bob observed that he might have to check the brakes on the old truck pretty soon, even as he scolded himself for taking his eyes off the road. Emily was still holding her printout, looking a little pale.

"Sorry about that," he told her. There at the stop sign he kept his foot on the brake and checked the rearview mirror to make sure no one was following. "Let's see what you got."

"This is the one I thought you'd like." She held it out for him to see. The photo caught him by surprise, honestly. He held it up close, and though it looked grainy and blurred, there was no mistaking.

"For a minute there, I thought . . ." He looked up at Emily's face again just to be sure he wasn't imagining things. But no, the resemblance was clear enough. "I almost thought I was looking at you."

"That's really funny, Grandpa." She took back the printout. "Ashley said the same thing."

"Well, honestly, I'd never realized it before just now. But you and your grandma could have been sisters."

"Weird, huh? But you must have seen that picture before. I mean the real picture."

"Not for a long time. I'd almost forgotten."

He looked from the fuzzy photo to his granddaughter's face once more, and a horn honked from behind them.

"Hey, hold your horses, okay?" Bob waved the driver around, and then changed his mind and hit the gas. Emily carefully put her project away as they neared home, and they talked about the harvest party and Sam's upcoming soccer game. Finally Emily cleared her throat and looked straight at her grandfather.

"Grandpa, can I ask you something?"

Well, of course she could, and he told her as much.

"You and Grandma have been married a long time, right?"

"You know we have."

"How many years again?"

"Let's see..." Bob really only had to do his mental math for a moment. "Forty-six years, I believe."

"Wow." Emily smiled and clutched her project to her chest as they pulled into the driveway. "I mean, I knew that, but still it's just totally cool, being married so long."

Totally cool. Bob supposed she was right. It was totally cool.

Chapter Twenty

Charlotte looked out the back-door window to see what was taking Bob so long to follow Emily inside. "I can't believe he actually drove," she said to herself, trying not to boil over. At the moment, though, Bob was just sitting in the cab of his truck, and it almost looked as if he were praying. Never mind the approaching dark. She stepped outside and walked toward the pickup.

"Bob?" She knocked on the window. "Are you all right?"

Bob jerked his head up and looked at her with surprise before rolling down the window.

"Look, I'm sorry," he began. He took the keys out of the ignition and handed them over to her. "I guess I was just trying to prove to myself that I wasn't, I don't know, completely helpless."

"You don't need to prove anything to me," she told him, accepting the keys. "I just don't want you doing anything that's not safe."

"We made it home fine. But I decided something."

She wondered what he was getting at but let him continue. He took a deep breath.

"I'll do it," he said.

"You'll do it," she repeated. "And what exactly—"

"I'll do the couples' seminar thing. Whatever we need to say, I'll put in my two cents, for what it's worth. I still don't know if anybody wants to hear it. But how hard can it be?"

She smiled and studied his face for a moment, the same face she had fallen in love with all those years ago. He raised his hand to grip hers.

"Thank you," she told him. "But what changed your mind?"

She followed his gaze as Emily popped her head out the back door to ask, "When's dinner going to be ready, Grandma?"

"Emily," she whispered.

"Yeah, that granddaughter of yours, she has a way of making a guy think."

Charlotte nodded. She knew exactly what he meant.

At the same time, she noticed Pete hurrying across the parking area to his apartment, and she couldn't let it pass.

"Peter Stevenson!" she shouted, and waved for him to join her at the back porch. "You come over here right now."

Pete paused for a moment before finally sidling up to the back step, where she stood with arms crossed.

"What'd I do?" he asked, preempting his mother.

"It's what you haven't done that's bothering me. Have you been eating?"

"Oh, Mom." He shook his head. "Not again."

"Pete, I just want to make sure you show up for dinner tonight."

"Well . . ." He would not be hard to convince. "I could use a square meal, I guess."

"And then after dinner maybe you could help your

father set up the firewood for the harvest party tomorrow night."

"I knew there would be a catch." He looked over his shoulder to see Bob approaching. Toby was in the tail-wagging, happy process of greeting everyone with a lick on the hand.

"Grandpa's in the doghouse." Emily chimed in. "He wasn't supposed to be driving, with his bad eyes."

"What doghouse are we talking about?" By now Bob was close enough to hear what they were all saying, but he just slipped past them and into the kitchen. Naturally he didn't take his boots off soon enough, and Toby added her own set of dusty paw prints to the mix. Instead of complaining, though, Charlotte couldn't keep from whispering an announcement to Pete and Emily: "Actually, he's not in the doghouse anymore. He said he would speak at the couples' seminar."

"What? No, he didn't." Pete's eyes widened. "Last time I mentioned it to him, he was definitely in the 'no way' column."

Now inside, they all stared at Bob washing his hands, as if watching a show or waiting for him to deny everything.

"What are you all looking at?" He turned around, his hands still dripping, but no one said anything else. Better not to.

Charlotte felt her cheeks flush but hurried to help Emily set another place at the table. Bob went into the family room to watch a little TV before dinner, and Pete followed him.

About an hour later, after Sam had returned from soccer practice, they all gathered around the table. After Bob said grace, they tucked into the meal and shared about their day. Charlotte was curious about Emily's wedding dress project.

"You still have those old photos, don't you?" Charlotte asked Emily.

"Er, sure." Emily didn't look quite so sure. "I'll get them back to you real soon."

"You do still have them?"

Emily looked off to the side, which could not have been a good sign.

"Uh, not exactly. I mean, they're somewhere. Just not... I'm sure I can find them."

"Don't tell me you lost them?" Charlotte tried not to let her voice get too loud.

"No—I mean, just temporarily. Not lost. Misplaced."

Christopher piped up. "I thought *misplaced* and *lost* meant the same thing."

"Hush." Emily gave her brother the evil eye. "Nobody asked you."

Now she looked back up at Charlotte with a plea in her expression. "I promise I'll get them back to you real soon, Grandma. Don't worry."

Charlotte wished she knew Emily's definition of *soon*, but by that time talk had turned back to the planned harvest party the next evening. Both Emily and Christopher promised to bring all their friends, and Charlotte once again made Pete promise to bring Dana.

"All right, all right," he told them, working through a mouthful of Charlotte's special wild-rice harvest casserole, with cream of mushroom soup, chicken, and cashews. "She's more excited about it than I am."

Only Sam remained quiet through the livelier-than-usual evening meal, not even complaining when he had to clear the dishes. Charlotte waited until the others had moved to the living room or upstairs before she approached him at the sink.

"You've been awfully quiet tonight," she told him. "Something on your mind? Did practice go all right?"

He nodded and lowered a saucepan into the sudsy hot water. But he wasn't going to get away with just a nod.

"How about school?" She tried again. "We don't hear much from you about your teachers or your classes."

"Classes are okay," he replied, and then paused a minute before sighing. "Coach said there might be some college scouts coming to our games."

"Oh!" She wasn't sure what to make of that. "That's good news, isn't it?"

"Mostly."

"Then why didn't you tell all of us at dinner, instead of me having to pry it out of you now?"

Sam shrugged and continued his scrubbing and carving up suds.

"We're just such losers." He paused again. "Even if they show up, and that's not for sure, it would be hard to get anybody's attention."

"You've said that before. It still doesn't sound like a great way to describe your team."

"But it's true. None of the guys know how to play, except..."

"Except you?"

"I wasn't going to say that."

"I hope not."

"Well, it's still pretty frustrating. If I could just get a scout's attention, that would totally be my ticket into college, like the U of N."

"Actually, I think getting good grades would totally be your ticket into college, no matter where you wanted to go. Which reminds me, how is it going getting those brochures together?"

Charlotte could tell by his suddenly soured expression that he didn't care much for the reminder.

"I don't need to get good grades to get into college," he told her, ducking the question. "Not if the scouts see me."

"Sam." She knew she wasn't making points with him now, but she had to say it. "You just can't depend on that kind of thing."

"Are you saying I can't do it? You saying I can't play?"

"No, that's not what I'm saying. We all know you're a gifted athlete. All I'm saying is that you shouldn't depend too much on the soccer. Give yourself some options."

"Options? Grandma, you don't get it. You don't understand."

"I understand that . . . no, all right. I suppose I don't understand anything at all."

Sam's sharp words set her back, so she pressed her lips together, not knowing what else to say. If he was going to be this stubborn, well, she couldn't make him do anything. It was his life.

Meanwhile Sam just scrubbed viciously at another pot, sending suds flying in every direction. He didn't look at her. So without another word she turned and left the kitchen before she did more damage.

Chapter Twenty-One

When Sam looked out of the corner of his eye at the bleachers behind him, he checked to see if Grandma or Grandpa might have arrived for the game.

They had a lot of work to do and weren't there. They always had a lot of work to do. And with the harvest party tonight, he couldn't expect them to drive all the way to Kearney on a Saturday morning for a dumb old soccer game, could he? When he had mentioned it yesterday, they promised they would make the next game.

As the game got under way, he fully expected the sky to open up. So far, only a drizzle gave the fans a reason to huddle under slickers and umbrellas. At least it wasn't as bone-chillingly cold as it could have been.

"Let's go!" He cheered on his teammates the way he knew he was supposed to. Too bad they were going to be trounced, and this was just the first half of the first game. At this rate, it was going to be a long, long season.

Especially sitting on this bench, which was so bogus he didn't have words for it. Jared Wilson, who was sitting next to him, leaned over and whispered in his ear. "See that guy over behind us wearing the Huskers cap?" asked Jared. "That's the U of N scout Coach was talking about."

"How do you know?" Sam wasn't about to turn and stare like a little kid, so he bent down and pretended to re-tie his shoelaces as he checked. Sure enough, a puffy-cheeked older guy with a red cap and blazer sat in the first row with a clipboard and a pair of binoculars, following some of the players.

Players on the other team, that is. As far as Sam was concerned, nobody on his own Harding Pioneers team would be worth recruiting to play college ball. On the other hand, a couple of forwards on the team from Kearney looked pretty decent. The Kearney Storm was already blowing them away.

"See him? Huh?" Jared jabbed Sam in the side with his elbow.

"Chill, would you? Yeah, I see him." But right now that wasn't really what caught his eye. Because behind the scout ... what? This time he couldn't help swiveling completely around for a better view.

Arielle?

She stood up to wave with both hands, and what could he do but wave back? Not that he didn't want to wave back. But the scout gave him a funny *Who are you?* look before he brought his binoculars back up to his eyes.

"Whoa," said Jared. "Why didn't you tell me you knew the guy?"

"I don't. My, uh ... a friend was waving from right behind him."

Jared wasn't at all shy about staring back at the crowd, no matter how uncool it looked. He had probably been one of those little kids who had to peek out through the curtains to see his parents in the audience at the school play. Right now, though, he didn't seem to know who Arielle was, until finally—

"Oh, you mean your *girl*friend! Why didn't you say so?"

"You didn't ask." Sam returned to following the game and cheering, even though he could see precious little out on the playing field to cheer about. Just minutes into the first half they already trailed Kearney two-zip. As they neared the end of the first half, the Storm rubbed it in by adding two more goals.

Meanwhile, Coach Mendenhall paced the sidelines like a caged lion, growling and yelling stuff that nobody out on the field would be able to understand. Heck, Sam and the other six benchwarmers were sitting just a few feet away from him, and even they couldn't make out what he was getting at—except that they should be doing something different out on the field.

All Sam knew was that he wanted to be out there showing what he could do. In fact, he needed to be out there before the scout got fed up and left. Judging by the frown on the guy's face, that could be soon.

Coach, come on! He could have screamed the words if it would have done any good, and he clenched his fists in frustration. *Put me in!*

"Doesn't do any good," Jared told him, crossing his arms across his chest as if he knew exactly what Sam was thinking. Well, why not? In the cursed Fellowship of the Benchwarmer, guys understood certain things about each other, and this was one of them.

By halftime Sam and the other benchwarmers were still

huddled on the bench, feeling miserable. What was the point? An angry gray sky now spit even more rain as Coach Mendenhall berated the starters for their mistakes before sending them back out to get pummeled in the second half.

"Coach?" Sam tried to catch his attention. He almost felt sorry for the man, just looking at the pain that worked its way across the wrinkles on his forehead, up and down. Coach threw both hands up when one of their players pirouetted less than gracefully and ended up on his back.

"Aw, come on, ref!" shouted the coach. "How about calling a foul there?"

"Coach?" Sam tried one more time. "Coach, how about putting me in?"

Coach Mendenhall didn't take his eyes off his players on the field, and didn't answer right away.

"You'll get your chance, Slater."

"But—" Sam sighed and thought he'd better not push things any more than he had. He'd get his chance? Not at this rate.

"What'd I tell you?" Jared told him. From one loser to the other. And the worst thing was, Sam was starting to believe he was a loser too.

Over in the stands the scout was still watching and scribbling notes. Late in the second half, by some miracle the Pioneers managed to slip in a wobbly goal behind a Storm defender.

Still the slaughter went on, with no relief in sight. Now they were so far behind Sam knew it wouldn't matter who they put in. A monkey or a four-year-old——no difference. He was afraid to look at Arielle, who faithfully cheered them on, but he couldn't help trading smiles with her every so often. A sliver of hope remained as long as the scout still sat in the front row with his binoculars.

Once again Sam did his best to catch the attention of his coach, who by this time mostly hung his head and shaded his eyes from the painful sight of his team being taken apart. Finally, with only a few minutes left in the game, he pointed at Sam.

"Coach?" Sam shed his jacket and expectantly trotted in place, warming up, until the coach grabbed him by the shoulder and talked into his face.

"You know why I haven't played you yet?"

Sam shook his head no, even though he knew all too well.

"'Cause you haven't shown me you're a team player yet, that's why. And I'd rather lose a game fifty-to-nothing than play a showboat."

Sam's mouth hung open, and he nearly bit his tongue when the coach slammed him on the back, sending him stumbling out into the slippery field.

"You're in for Miller. Now just remember what I said," Coach shouted.

The referee motioned for Sam to come into the game as little Aaron Miller trotted off the field, trading places with Sam, who raced into position, looking totally out of place with his fresh-from-the-laundry, blue-and-white uniform in the sea of muddy ones. That would change pretty quickly. Less than five minutes were left in the game.

Take a look, Mr. Scout! He shivered as he imagined the man had his binoculars trained right at him. In any case, Arielle was watching, for sure. That counted for something.

At first his nerves got the better of him. He couldn't get to a couple of weak passes, tripped a few times, and generally didn't do what he knew he could do. In the short time they had left he would have to ratchet up his game, or else.

But first he would have to get the ball. And with Harding's crumbled, demoralized defense, the other team controlled the ball. It didn't even get close to Sam. How could they ever score a goal if they didn't get the ball up to his end of the field?

"Come on, guys!" Sam added his shout to the din as sleet made the field more slippery. "Give us a chance up here!"

Well, they couldn't have heard him. But a few seconds later he suddenly found the ball bouncing his way, spinning in the mud. Finally a chance to show what he could do!

With the crowd cheering, he pivoted and dribbled through two defenders, calling up all the ball-handling skills he could muster. Two of his teammates woke up enough to join him as he approached the opposing goal. Now! They finally had a chance to redeem themselves in the final minutes with a respectable goal.

He slipped by another defender, bringing the ball closer still. Coach Mendenhall screamed something, and Sam looked for a clear path. If he could get by the last two Kearney defenders, he could tap it into the goal himself.

On the other hand, his teammate Josh now waved from the middle of the field, just as he always did in practice. He might have a clear shot.

All right, Josh, he thought. *I don't know why I'm doing this, but . . .*

He passed the ball to the middle just the way Coach Mendenhall had demanded, giving Josh his chance. Then he gritted his teeth, waiting to see. He almost couldn't watch.

Josh bobbled and hesitated long enough for the Kearney defender to catch up to him and strip away the ball. And that was it. End of story. Sam groaned to see the ball once more sailing the wrong way as the whistle blew to end the game.

Josh looked good and beat but held out his hand as he trudged past Sam. That was the first time any of his teammates had done that.

"Nice pass, buddy." Josh wiped the mud from his face and flashed a tired grin. "I thought you were going to take it in yourself."

"Well, you know, I guess that's not the play."

"So next time I won't blow it. I promise."

Speaking of blowing it, Sam glanced over at the scout. Sure enough, the man headed straight across the field to talk to the Kearney coach. That figured. He would not be having any conversations with anyone on the hapless Harding team.

But what could Sam do about it now? He didn't mind the pats on the back he got from his teammates, or even the thumbs up from Coach Mendenhall, which was better than he'd gotten from him in a long time. But the best part was having Arielle run up next to him on the way to the parking lot.

"That was a really nice play," she told him. Coming from Arielle, it sounded a whole lot better than if one of the guys had said it. "You should have heard what the people around me said."

"Yeah?"

"They said you'd never pass it, that you always . . . well, that you always hog the ball."

"Maybe I should have. But I had to surprise 'em, right?"

When Arielle laughed, Sam was sure everything was worth it—getting soaked in the rain, losing, maybe even missing out on the chance to impress that college scout.

"You want to ride home with me?" she asked. "I mean, unless you drove yourself."

"Actually, I rode the bus here to Kearney with the other guys. Left my car in the Harding High parking lot."

"I could take you back there."

No way was he going to argue.

"Well . . . sure. I just have to tell them. Be right back."

A minute later he trotted back and climbed into the already-warming cab of Arielle's dad's truck.

"You sure it's not out of your way?" he asked.

He knew it was, considering where the Friesens lived, on the other side of Bedford from Heather Creek Farm, about five miles out on Highway 4. But Arielle didn't seem to mind as they left the parking lot and headed home.

The windshield wipers made most of the noise for the first several minutes, until Arielle finally pointed to a large envelope on the dash.

"Actually, Sam, that's for you."

Sam fingered the large envelope bearing the UNIVERSITY OF NEBRASKA, LINCOLN logo, a little unsure of what she meant. His puzzled look must have told her so.

"It's nothing," she told him. "Just an extra application I got. Some catalogs and stuff. I thought maybe you'd be interested. Heard they had a pretty decent soccer team."

"Yeah, that's what I heard too." He pulled out the glossy color brochures, which he had seen before but never really paid attention to. Until now. "You don't know who was sitting in front of you at the game, right?"

"I heard about the scout," she said. "He'll be back."

"Maybe." He leafed through the catalog and thanked her for thinking of him.

Sam couldn't keep his eyes off her seriously beautiful eyes and the little button of a nose, the cheeks that had turned a shade of pink—just the way they did in class. "Thanks for coming too. It was really nice to have a cheering section."

"I had fun." She smiled and peeked at him out of the corner of her eye, and he liked the tingly feeling of sitting in the truck with her, bumping along country roads. He liked the very faint smell of her perfume that lingered in the warmth of the cab, though it made him wonder. *She put that on for watching soccer games?*

"You like the Huskers, don't you?" she asked, keeping her eyes on the road.

"Well, if I went to the school, guess I'd have to, right?"

"That would be a requirement, all right."

He leafed through the catalog some more, checking out the computer programming and Web design stuff as well as the athletics pages. It didn't look half bad, actually. And if Arielle ended up going there too, that could be a bonus.

Chapter Twenty-Two

Christopher held his breath as his Uncle Pete came in close to Mr. Pumpkin with the loader attached to the back of his tractor. This thing could squash the poor deformed masterpiece, easy. So he parked himself on his knees right next to the beach-ball-size pumpkin, waving Uncle Pete closer.

"Careful!" he cried out. "Just a few more inches. Careful!"

Grandpa crouched on the other side, waving his own instructions, so Uncle Pete had plenty of help. He leaned back in the tractor seat, moving the controls a little at a time.

"Two more inches!" yelled Christopher. "There!"

Uncle Pete slipped the scooper into the dirt and vines underneath Mr. Pumpkin and revved the engine. A few seconds later he had it safely inside the scooper, and a few seconds after that he'd unloaded their prizewinner into the back of his truck. Piece of cake, right? Christopher jumped up to make sure.

"How are you doing, huh, Mr. Pumpkin?"

Mr. Pumpkin looked just as solid there in the back of the truck as he had all these weeks in the secret pumpkin patch. Christopher wiped a little dirt off the side of the pumpkin with a rag, even though it was going to take a lot more than that to make this thing pretty.

"Whew!" Uncle Pete stepped up to the side of the truck after he'd shut off his tractor. "I'm glad this isn't going to be a beauty contest. Looks like that thing of yours has a bad rash."

"Doesn't matter how ugly it is," said Grandpa, slamming the tailgate shut. "All it has to do is weigh more than everybody else's. Right, Christopher? Ready to go enter the contest?"

"I'm going to ride back here," announced Christopher, but Uncle Pete just scooped him up the way he had the giant pumpkin and scooted him into the cab between himself and Grandpa.

"Sorry, dude. You might bounce out and then we'd never find you again. But you can ride up here with Grandpa."

Well, Christopher figured that was okay too—as long as the pumpkin didn't start rolling around. Luckily the big orange and yellow and splotchy green pumpkin stayed pretty much where they'd set it all the way into town. Uncle Pete took the corners pretty slow.

When they got close to the *Bedford Leader* newspaper office, Christopher pointed out the small crowd of people already milling around on the sidewalk, and several pickups backed up to unload. Four men muscled a pretty large pumpkin down to the sidewalk right in front of the brick building. It looked like one of those perfect Halloween pumpkins. The newspaper editor, Mr. Barnes, was rolling a big scale down the sidewalk, like the kind they used at the feed store.

"One, two, three . . ." Christopher counted five other pumpkins already. Each one looked . . . He gulped. They all looked pretty big.

"Don't worry, dude." Uncle Pete didn't sound worried. "They don't have a chance against yours."

Well, he hoped not. Now a banner had been hoisted across the front of the building, just above the front doors: BEDFORD LEADER GIANT PUMKIN CONTEST.

"Did they misspell that on purpose?" wondered Christopher out loud.

"What?" Maybe Uncle Pete didn't see it. He was busy parking the truck so they could unload. Christopher supposed the four strong guys would lift theirs off too. That seemed a little risky, though, considering Uncle Pete had loaded it with the backhoe. But maybe it would be okay.

Grandpa rubbed the Saturday morning stubble on his chin. "Looks like we're not the only ones entering the contest."

"Doesn't matter," said Uncle Pete as he backed the truck up to the sidewalk one door down from the office. "All those other folks spent all their time growing a pretty pumpkin, huh? Ours is big, fat, and ugly."

Christopher grinned at his uncle and grandpa on either side of him, and then he didn't feel quite as nervous. Yeah. Big, fat, and ugly. As long as they didn't drop it on the sidewalk, maybe they had a chance.

"HOW ABOUT THAT?" Charlotte smiled as she peered out her kitchen window early Saturday evening. "Looks like we'll be spared any rain tonight."

Good thing too. The weather was the one thing she couldn't control. By then Charlotte was pretty sure she had everything else under control for the harvest party. Except perhaps her husband's attitude.

"Let's see..." She went down her mental checklist. Four large packages of marshmallows and enough chocolate and graham crackers for s'mores? Check. Christopher had already called dibs on one whole package for himself. They would see about that.

Wood for the fire, arranged teepee-style in a fire pit at the edge of the parking area, along with kindling and matches? Check. She'd convinced Pete to dig the pit this morning, and he hadn't resisted.

Several gallons of fresh local apple cider, ready for heating on the stove? Check. She couldn't wait to linger over the heavenly steam above the kettle.

Now all they needed was guests, most of whom were expected shortly.

Bob emerged from the nearest cornfield on his oldest tractor, and he didn't look like a happy camper as he shut down his rig next to the back porch. The tractor sputtered just like its owner. He looked at Charlotte and dusted off his flannel shirt with his cap.

"Good thing the harvest is winding up pretty soon, or I wouldn't have had time for this thing."

Charlotte wondered how much time it could really have taken to help prepare a bonfire, but she just let him complain.

"Wonder if anybody's going to show up for Emily's party anyway."

"Don't dampen her plans, Bob."

"Who, me?" He held up his hands in surrender. "I'm cooperating. I'm along for the ride."

"Well, okay, but that reminds me: Where did you and Pete go this morning with Christopher? It looked as if you had something big in the back of the truck."

"Oh, that. That was nothing."

"It was something."

"Look, I can't tell you. It's just something me and the kid have been working on, and if he wants to tell you, he's going to do it himself."

"I thought we didn't have secrets in this family."

Well, she would find out in time. But right now she returned to the kitchen, where over the next little while she would gather her supplies and double-check to make sure they had enough grilling dogs, buns, condiments, and paper plates.

A few minutes later Pete burst into the kitchen wearing jeans and a ripped white T-shirt with a Youth Blast '99 logo on the chest. That old shirt was ready for the rag bag.

"You seen that stack of wood Dad put up for the fire?" His cheeks looked rosy and he puffed a bit from the running around. "Pretty good work for a blind man, huh?"

"That's no way to talk about your father." She pointed at his shirt. "And what do you think this is, summer?"

He grinned at her.

"Indian summer, Momma dear. You been outside lately? Full moon coming up. Must be at least sixty or sixty-five. Now that's what I'm talking about!"

Aside from calling her "Momma dear" she didn't mind seeing him a little happier—compared to the way he'd been moping around lately. Maybe he'd gotten over whatever it was that had been bothering him. She couldn't bring herself to ask, but mentioned it to Bob a few minutes later when Pete was out of earshot.

"A better mood?" Bob set down a couple packages of paper napkins on the counter. "Not sure what you mean."

"Don't tell me it's another one of your father and son secrets." She handed him two large bags of chips to take outside. "Let me guess: Did you agree to the windmill?"

"Not yet. We'll decide after that Justin fellow collects his data."

She would have asked more questions, but Bob slipped out too quickly. And by that time people had begun to arrive, starting with her son Bill and his wife, Anna. She wanted to see how pregnant Anna was looking at seven months along. She waved at Anna to join her in the kitchen while the girls, Madison and Jennifer, ran to watch Bob and Pete lighting the fire.

Anna did step inside, though she didn't seem quite as pleased to be there as did the rest of the family.

"If anyone tells me I'm positively glowing," Anna announced with a straight face and a raised hand of warning, "I'm going to be ill."

"How about some hot cider?" Charlotte ladled steaming, aromatic cider into mugs for Bill's family as a line of pickups pulled into the drive, lights blinking and horns blazing.

"Everybody's here!" announced Christopher, poking his head in the kitchen door.

"Think I'd better go direct traffic," said Bill, squaring his small town mayor's shoulders. That left Charlotte and Anna in the kitchen with platters of food and goodies yet to take outside. Before they could do that, however, Hannah arrived.

"There you are, stranger!" Charlotte gave her friend a big hug. How long had it been? "I have so missed our walks!"

"Me too, honey. Me too."

Charlotte gave her another hug for good measure. "How's Frank's mother?" she asked.

"A little better. I was beginning to think I'd have to move to Lincoln for a while to take better care of her. You know how those rest homes are. I hope I never—"

She caught herself in midsentence.

"I'm sorry, Char. I almost forgot where you've been working lately. Not all nursing homes are that bad. You know what I mean."

"Of course I do. I'm just so glad to see you. And we've been praying for her at church."

The friends exchanged news about life and worries, and soon it came around to Bob's upcoming operation.

"They say it's quite routine," said Charlotte, stirring her cider as they spoke, "and that they perform this procedure all the time now. I hope they're right."

"It's wonderful what they can do these days."

"Well, yes. But even so, I think Bob's quite nervous about it. He hasn't wanted to talk about it at all."

"You can't blame him. You don't seem too calm and collected about it, yourself."

"I'm trying to encourage him. From everything we've been told, the laser surgery is just a simple outpatient procedure, so he doesn't even stay in the hospital overnight. And they say there may be just a little soreness, but that he should be back to normal in a matter of days."

"I'm sure that's a relief to you, dear, especially with the harvest and the kids."

"You have no idea."

They finally turned to where Anna stood awkwardly by the sink, delicately holding a sponge with two fingers and dragging it around the counter.

"Oh, dear," said Hannah, "and here we are, gabbing away like we haven't seen each other in years. Wouldn't you rather sit down, dear?"

"Hannah's right." Charlotte looked at her very pregnant daughter-in-law and tried to escort her outside with everyone else. "We've set up lawn chairs by the fire where it's warm."

"Actually, I'm not cold at all." Anna pulled her lovely cream-colored cashmere sweater more closely around her, picked up one of the platters piled high with Hershey's chocolate and graham crackers, and headed for the door. "Just tell me where you want this."

"Out on the picnic table would be fine." Charlotte pointed out the two tables near the blazing bonfire, and Anna hurried outside. By then the yard was full of happy teenagers, most of them still celebrating how the Bedford High football team had drubbed their unlucky opponent by a lopsided margin—twenty-eight to three. Charlotte noticed Emily's friends Ashley, Megan, and Hunter out there as well as Sam's buddies Jake and Paul, and Arielle.

"I'm sorry," Hannah told Charlotte. "Did I say something wrong?"

"No need to apologize." Charlotte slipped an arm around her friend's waist as they headed outside themselves with marshmallows and skewers. She dodged Toby, who had skittered through the door ahead of them, and lowered her voice. "You didn't say anything wrong. Anna's just like that sometimes. Especially now that she's expecting."

"I understand," Hannah replied. "Or actually, maybe you understand that state of mind better than I do."

They both had a good giggle. Even so, Charlotte would track Anna down later to make sure everything was all right. Arm in arm she and Hannah stepped out into the warm evening.

Outside, it was hard not to catch the enthusiasm of the kids as they gathered around the bonfire. Before long, Jason Vink, the church's youth group leader, started singing an off-key version of the Bedford High fight song, giving them all a great excuse to join in. Then the ring of young people laughed and talked as they held flaming marshmallows a little too close to the bonfire.

"Here, look," Bob said as golden flames licked higher and higher and pungent wood smoke drifted high into the flickering circle of light above their heads. "You gotta wait till it dies down a little more. Then you can brown 'em right over the coals."

"Where's the fun in that, Grandpa?" asked Sam. Charlotte noticed Arielle sitting awfully close to him. Dana had just arrived, as well, though Charlotte tried not to stare as she greeted Pete in the flickering shadows beyond the fire. They looked very happy to see each other.

"Bob seems to be enjoying himself," whispered Hannah,

and Charlotte nodded her agreement. For now. Maybe he had set aside all the things they'd been concerned about, the way men seemed to do. She leaned against a nearby elm and enjoyed the warmth radiating from the campfire.

For one perfect moment, as young people laughed and sparks flew upward toward a full harvest moon, Charlotte wished she could imagine that everything was right in her little world—even if it wasn't.

Chapter Twenty-Three

Pete looked over his shoulder, back at the bonfire, and shoved his hands into his jeans pockets as he and Dana escaped the party and headed down the path toward Heather Creek.

"I'm just really glad you decided to come out for the harvest party tonight," he told Dana, pulling his hands back out and crossing his arms on his chest.

"Well, of course I wanted to come out, silly." Dana chuckled and looked over at him. Moonlight made her beautiful smile shine. "Why wouldn't I?"

"I don't know; you've got a lot going at school."

"Not more than usual."

"But you're really plugged into that world, aren't you?"

"What do you mean, 'plugged in'?"

"Nothing. I just mean, well . . ." He struggled for the right words, not finding them. "I mean, you probably couldn't imagine living on a farm like this."

"What in the world are you talking about?" She pulled back to look at him in the moonlight. "Pete, I love this place. I have always loved this place. I thought you knew that. The horses, the barns, the creek ... even the people."

"Oh, well, glad you included that last part." He laughed nervously. "For a minute I wasn't so sure."

Now he could hide his nerves behind lighthearted banter, and she took his arm as they continued down the path. Good thing the moon lit their way; it was so bright it even cast blue shadows between the thinning tree branches overhead as they neared the cottonwoods that wrapped Heather Creek in their embrace. As Pete and Dana drew closer, dry leaves crackled underfoot.

"Are you cold?" She looked at him sideways and leaned a little closer. "You're shaking. Maybe we should go back to the fire."

"No, no, not cold. I'm fine. I'm good. Not cold."

Maybe she knew him better than that. She didn't sound convinced.

"Then what? You've been acting a little strange the past couple of days."

"Strange?"

"Yeah, you know. Jumpy. Moody. Distant. Is something bothering you?"

"Uh." By this time his tongue felt like it was beginning to stick to the roof of his mouth. That, and his pulse rate was starting to rev up, no matter how much he told himself to calm down.

"Is that all you can say? Huh? Pete, maybe you're coming down with something."

"I'm not sick."

"What then? Is there, is there something you want to ... ask me?"

"Uh ..." Once more the words froze in his mouth before he could release them, and she questioned him again.

"Pete, if you and I have a future, we can't keep secrets, right?"

"Secrets? You think we've got a—"

He was about to say future when he felt the leaves under his feet give way, like thin ice on a not-quite-frozen pond. He tried to catch his balance, but he couldn't help slipping down a short embankment toward the creek, pulling Dana with him. The carpet of leaves made the bank as slick as ice.

"Hold on!" he cried, but really there wasn't much to do except slide feet-first to the bottom of the gully, about ten feet. Dana did hold on to his arm, laughing all the way. Moments later they came to a stop in a pile of leaves, just a few feet from the banks of gurgling Heather Creek.

"Are you all right?" asked Pete. He tried to help Dana to her feet, but only slipped again. And she fell into his arms laughing.

"That was a great ride," she replied between laughs. Once he knew she hadn't gotten hurt he couldn't help but join in the laughter too.

Just to be sure he hadn't lost anything, though, he reached down to his pocket. The ring was still there, just as it had been for the past several days. Only this time, maybe he could rouse the courage to pull it out and actually present it to her, here in the "Engagement Spot" Dad had always told him about.

He finally helped her to her feet and told her he was okay. If only he really were. Surely she could hear his heart beating out of his chest, even over the light rustle of leaves in the breeze overhead, the soft burble of water behind them, and the distant voices and laughter around the bonfire.

Now or never, he told himself, holding her hand and lowering himself to one knee—although he kind of fell to the side and sat down. In the distance, he thought he heard someone calling, and he lost his bearings again in the dark and the leafy carpet. Well, it was slippery, but never mind.

"Pete, you *did* hurt yourself." Her voice turned serious. She crouched down to get a better look. "And you're still shaking like crazy."

"Dana!" He held on to her hand. With her head silhouetted in a shaft of moonlight streaming in from between the trees, he could see several leaves still stuck in her hair. "I'm not hurt, and I don't need to go back to the house. I just need to ask you something."

"Oh! Well, actually I was hoping you did." Her voice softened. "Though I still don't know what we're doing down here on the ground."

Once again he heard the distant voice, only this time it wasn't nearly so distant. And this time, he could tell who it belonged to.

Christopher.

Honestly, Pete would have hidden behind a tree if he could have, or under a pile of leaves.

"Oh, no," he whispered, hoping Christopher wouldn't discover them. "Dana, shh! Don't say a word."

"Uncle PEEETE!" Amazing how such a loud sound could come from such a small body, just above their heads. "Uncle Pete! Where are you?"

Christopher didn't have to wonder very long, as he

himself came tumbling down into the little gully the same way they both had. He landed in a heap right next to them.

"Whoa!" said Christopher, jumping to his feet. "That was cool! I'm going to try that again sometime."

"Christopher!" Pete grabbed for his nephew's arm but missed. "What are you doing down here?"

"Looking for you, whaddya think? I saw you guys sneaking off, so I knew where you were. But Uncle Pete, you'll never believe it!"

Pete sighed and tried to keep from sounding completely annoyed.

"What do you need, Christopher?"

Any other time! Couldn't Christopher have come bumbling down into the gully any other time?

Christopher grabbed Pete's arm in his excitement. "Come on, I have to show you!"

"Hold on." Pete pulled back. "Could we do this some other time?"

"It's okay, Pete." Dana should not have said that. But this time there was no escape, so Pete let himself be pulled up the side of the gully and back toward the bonfire, and Dana followed along too. He thought he heard her sigh. But whether they liked it or not, his private-eye nephew was hot on the trail of something, and they were along for the ride.

"THERE, SEE?" Christopher pointed to the back of the shiny black dually pickup parked next to the barn, the one with two tires on each side of the back end for added support. "It's the exact same tire tracks I saw up by the . . . you know."

"You mean, up by your pumpkin patch?" asked Pete, stooping to see the tires Christopher was so excited about. The orange-and-gold light from the bonfire, bigger than ever, flickered over this way enough for them to get a pretty good look.

"Yeah, Christopher, it's a dually. So what? Some farms need that kind of truck to haul a big load or tow a trailer."

"That's what I mean." Christopher looked around as if Pete had just let out the biggest secret of the decade. "The tire tracks me and Dylan saw. I'll bet you anything it was the same truck."

Pete smiled when he saw the logo and company name on the side door. Was that all? They must have taken a look at the land before Pete even spoke with Justin. Mystery solved.

"You may be right, Christopher. I told Justin he could measure how much wind we have on our property."

"Justin?" Now Christopher's face drew a total blank. "Who's Justin?"

"Hey, gentlemen!" Justin Landwehr from TurboGen stepped up just then to say hi. He smiled as he extended his hand to Pete. "Glad I caught up to you. I was just finishing up my readings on your back acres this afternoon, picking up my equipment, like I said, and I thought I would check in with you before I headed back to Omaha. Took a little longer than I thought though. Didn't mean to crash your party."

"Not at all," replied Pete. "I'm glad you stopped by. Who can resist a s'more, right? So how does it look?"

"Actually, a little better than I expected. Must be something about the topography, but you've had some pretty steady breezes here. At least while I've been around. I still have to crunch some numbers, but I think a turbine would go real well up on that rise, just like we were saying."

Pete still didn't want to commit to the guy, but this was sounding pretty good. "Well, my dad and I have been thinking it over, and I've got to tell you we're still not sure about it. But I think we can make a decision pretty soon."

"That's all I can ask for," replied Justin.

Dana had strolled on back to the bonfire group while Pete and Christopher discussed the truck tires. Now she glanced back at Pete with a smile and waved.

"Oh, sorry. Justin, this is my nephew Christopher. Actually, Christopher's the family weather expert. He's even put together some of his own instruments. Very impressive for a fifth grader."

"Sixth." Christopher corrected him.

"Sixth. I knew that. Anyway, Christopher might be able to tell you something about the wind speeds up on that rise."

"No kidding?" Justin looked interested as he shook Christopher's hand. "I'd like to see your instruments sometime."

That scored a point or two with Christopher.

"Justin works for a company that puts up windmills on farms," continued Pete. "He's been checking things out around here, seeing what kind of wind we have."

"Yeah, in fact . . ." Justin reached into the cab of his big truck and pulled out a glossy brochure for Christopher.

"Here. This is the brochure I give people. You're welcome to it, seeing how you're into weather and stuff."

"Cool, thanks." Christopher took the brochure, which was filled with photos of TurboGen windmills and charts filled with wind speeds and generating capacities. Justin apparently knew how to get a kid's interest. He winked at Pete.

"I've got nephews, too. But look, I'm interrupting here. Didn't mean to do that. I'll e-mail you when I get back to my office, okay?"

"Sure." That was fine with Pete. But right now his mom and Dana were waving at them from over at the bonfire.

"Pete!" His mom called out. "Bring your friend over for some cider and s'mores!"

"Oh, actually, I . . ." Justin hemmed and hawed for a moment, but he wasn't jumping back into his truck right away either.

"Come on," Pete told him. "You can talk to my dad again too. Give him your best sales pitch."

"Er, actually, I'm not sure—"

"No, really. He'll be nice to you this time."

Pete dragged Justin over to the fire where they loaded him up with graham crackers, marshmallows, and chocolate. Amazing there was anything left, considering all the kids who had shown up. Charlotte just kept coming with more and more food, bowls of chips and cups of steaming cider, and now even hot dogs and buns. Like they needed to eat another entire meal.

While Justin and Christopher and all the others chowed down on more goodies, Dana slipped her hand into Pete's as they stood by the fire. "Maybe we can finish our conversation soon?" she whispered, checking her watch. "I hate to say it, but I have to get going."

Had she figured out the obvious? In an instant he felt the sweat on his forehead and a cold chill creeping up his spine. He'd come so close tonight, but missed. Yeah, well, baseball was a lot like that too. Strike two.

"Sure," he told her, keeping his voice steady. He'd have another chance. Maybe he'd even dig that silly how-to-propose booklet out of the trash again. He walked her to her car, and they said good night.

Chapter Twenty-Four

Emily paced the kitchen late the next Tuesday afternoon, wondering why she felt so helpless. The brochure on laser eye surgery made everything look so much more serious than the way Grandma had described it last night. She turned back to the living room, waving the brochure at her little brother.

"Christopher, did Grandma say anything else about this eye surgery? How long it was supposed to take, or anything like that? I would think they would be home by now."

"I don't know." Christopher shrugged, but then must have changed his mind because he turned to her from where he was working on a drawing at the kitchen table. "All I heard is what you heard. About the lasers and stuff. Grandma said it would be no big deal, right?"

"Yeah. No big deal." Emily wondered how serious this really was. What if something went wrong, and Grandpa went *really* blind? The thought gave her shivers as she wandered back into the kitchen looking for a snack. She sat down at the table with some chips and salsa. Despite her own fears about getting in trouble for losing Grandma's precious pictures, she couldn't help worrying about her grandfather instead.

"God, please don't let Grandpa go blind," she prayed, meaning every word of it as Uncle Pete made his usual entrance before dinnertime.

"Hey, you all," he told them with a smile, tossing his coat over a kitchen chair. "What's for dinner?"

He stopped to sniff when no one answered right away, and then wrinkled his nose. "Nobody here, huh?"

Christopher crumpled his drawing and looked up with worried eyes. "They're not home yet and we don't know what's taking them so long. Maybe something went wrong and the surgery didn't work the way it was supposed to. Maybe the lasers—"

"Relax, kid. There's nothing to worry about." Uncle Pete straightened up and ruffled Christopher's hair. "Sam will be home from soccer practice any minute, and he'll probably be starving. Let's see if there's something in the fridge we can heat up."

CHARLOTTE'S STUBBORN HUSBAND waved her off as she tried to open the car door for him on the way out of the eye clinic. A harvest moon had just risen over the surrounding fields, lending a bronze glow to the early evening. Had it really taken this long? Not the procedure itself, which the doctor said went just as advertised. Mostly the waiting had taken so long, and they were the last patients of the day to leave the clinic.

"Don't know why you're driving us home," he grumbled as he climbed into the passenger side. Once she had taken her place behind the steering wheel of her little Ford he held up a post-op care brochure for her to see. "Says here, 'After laser surgery for cataracts, most patients can resume their normal everyday activities immediately, including work, hobbies, driving, or shopping.'"

"You mean you want to go shopping?" As Charlotte started the car she thought she would try a gentle tease to see if he would push back. "Maybe this laser really did clear up your eyesight."

"All right, so let's go home," he replied, fastening his seat belt. "It's getting late."

Yes, they would do that, after they stopped by the pharmacy to pick up the eyedrops Bob would have to use for several days. She glanced at the brochure to see what he was reading. "It also says that most people experience only minor soreness," she told him, remembering what she had read earlier, "and that they usually go home to rest for the remainder of the day."

"That's just on account of the stuff they gave me for the pain."

"The anesthesia."

"Right. We'll see how much rest I need."

"You could actually read that, couldn't you?"

"Copyright Laser Eye Center of Harding," he said, holding up the brochure to the interior light. "All rights reserved. Telephone four-oh-two..."

"Well, there you go! You can even read the fine print! Was that really anything you needed to avoid, all this time? Now you won't have any trouble with the..."

She was about to say "with the seminar," but couldn't. Because even just thinking about how unprepared they were—well, it gave her a headache. She could deal with that later. One thing at a time. Right now she just needed to get her husband home, and see how the kids were doing.

The kids! They were probably wondering what had taken so long. Were they worried? Or maybe they hadn't even noticed how late it was getting. Either way, it would have been nice to have one of those cell phones right now.

ANY OTHER TIME, Emily would have avoided at any cost the so-called "dinner" Uncle Pete and Christopher had cooked up. Her stomach would have rebelled, her taste buds would have refused, and her head would have told her there was no nutritional value in scrambled eggs and canned ravioli, not to mention that other fried thing they'd added.

But tonight she just sat quietly at the kitchen table and waited for Grandma to get home with Grandpa, nibbling at the eggs and picking out the chunks of Spam. The boys, on the other hand, were oohing and ahhing and pouring more ketchup on their disgusting mounds of food.

"Now *that's* what I'm talking about." Uncle Pete pointed with satisfaction at another forkload of eggs-Spam-ravioli. "How often do you get a dinner like this? Huh?"

"Yeah!" Christopher nodded with enthusiasm. "This is great."

"Mmm-hmm." Sam shoveled another load into his own hungry mouth. He hadn't even bothered to take off his muddy soccer jersey, which Grandma would have insisted on if she were here. But she wasn't, of course. And here at this table, Emily knew she was outnumbered. She didn't even try to play her girl card. Instead she washed down her eggs with another sip of milk and waited until a pair of headlights finally flashed up the driveway several minutes later.

"They're here!" yelled Christopher. "It's Grandma and..."

But his voice dropped off as he looked more closely. Emily could tell it was someone else too. A wheezing old pickup, almost as old as Uncle Pete's.

"Wonder who that is," said Uncle Pete, pushing his chair out. A few seconds later they all watched as an older man—perhaps in his early seventies and bald as a billiard ball—stood on the back step and knocked on the door. Uncle Pete opened it.

"Well, look who's here," said Uncle Pete, shaking the man's hand. "Eddie. How are you? Come on in. You want some eggs and Spam?"

"Ah, no thanks." Eddie the janitor scraped a bit of mud off the toe of his sneaker. What in the world was he doing here? "Don't want to interrupt your dinner."

"Not at all," insisted Uncle Pete. "You come on in."

"No, actually, I just came to give you folks this." He held out a familiar-looking manila envelope, except that it had been stamped with a large footprint. Emily gasped when she recognized what it was.

"See, at first I had no idea who this belonged to," Eddie explained, "since it turned up in the trash. I figure some kids must have found it and tossed it there, so the envelope's been pretty well trampled. Got a little ketchup stain on it too, but what's inside is okay. Though I sure don't know how these old photographs found their way to school in the first place."

"Old photographs?" Uncle Pete scratched his head as he apparently tried to figure out what was going on here.

"Oh, Eddie!" Emily jumped to her feet. "I can't believe you found this. Thank you, thank you, thank you!"

"Well, you know." He chuckled as he handed it over. "They looked so much like you, Emily. But then I saw your grandmother's name on the back of one of them, really faint, in the corner. At first I thought it might be a picture of you."

"Let me see that." This time Uncle Pete took the photos and held one up next to Emily's face. "*Hmm*. Yup."

"I don't think they look like Emily," said Christopher, still eating. "Or like Grandma."

"They're really pretty pictures anyway," said Eddie. "Hope you didn't need them for a class or anything."

"They're for a report on Thursday. But I didn't need them anymore. Grandma did." Emily might have hugged him right there except that he backed away and sort of ducked his head with a shy smile.

"Well, anyway, I was on my way to my sister's house down the road. Glad we got them back to the right place."

"You have no idea, Eddie." Emily stood by the door and watched him retreat to his truck. "No idea."

And twenty minutes later, Emily still had no idea what was taking Grandma and Grandpa so long. Finally another pair of headlights bounced up the drive. It had to be.

"Is it them this time?" asked Christopher.

Emily waited until she was sure she recognized Grandma's car before giving a nod.

"It's them."

"Yes!" Christopher dropped his fork and flew for the door. Emily was right on his heels, and she didn't mind elbowing Sam out of the way to get through the back door. But within sight of Grandma's car she slowed down to a cool walk, letting Sam bound past her as they opened the car door to see what had happened to Grandpa. Never mind that when she looked down at her feet, she still wore her socks but no shoes.

"Well, that's quite a welcome home," said Grandma, climbing out of the driver's side. Even Uncle Pete came out to help his dad unfold his frame from the little car.

"So I thought you were going to come back with bandages all over your eyes," said Uncle Pete.

Grandpa frowned at him. "Who said anything about bandages? Just a couple laser shots, and that's all there was to it. They say I'll be back to doing all my normal chores in a day or two. So let's not fuss."

"Great!" Pete held up three fingers in front of his dad's face. "So how many fing—"

"Would you cut it out!" Grandpa batted Uncle Pete's hand out of the way. But Emily saw Grandpa smile as they trooped back into the house.

"Is that dinner I smell?" Grandma always had the best nose.

"Oh, yeah," said Christopher as they filed inside. "Uncle Pete made the grossest stuff!"

Chapter Twenty-Five

"Last row," Pete announced to himself as he turned the corner in his combine and aimed toward what was left of his standing corn.

Not that anyone would hear, but he allowed himself a little "Yeehaw!" and a pat on the back. Considering the harvest party the other night, all the drama with Dad's operation the day before, and the whole thing about the couples' seminar next Saturday, he thought he'd done pretty well to finish as quickly as he had, ahead of the expected rains. But what was this, Wednesday afternoon? Okay, not bad.

But then there was the thing with Dana.

Rather, the *fiasco* with Dana. So far he hadn't been able to come up with any great ideas to rebound from his botched proposal attempt. But he would think of something. He had to.

All he knew was the skywriting proposal was definitely out. On an overcast day like today, it wouldn't work anyway. And so were most of the other awful public proposals suggested in his awful wedding-proposals book, which he had finally put to rest for good. What made those guys think the whole world needed to see WILL YOU MARRY ME? the same time as she did?

No, thank you. He'd pretty much decided the proposal would have to be classy, private, and soon. Otherwise, if Dana had any clue of what was brewing (which he assumed she did by now), or if too much time went by, she would figure out just how much of a coward he really was. Or maybe she would go looking for a better offer, like from one of her school friends with a Volvo and a Ph.D.

What was he waiting for?

As if to answer the question, he could see someone pushing a wheelbarrow across the field maybe a hundred yards ahead and just off to the left, at the end of his cornrow. He couldn't be sure yet, but it looked as if he or she was headed straight toward the last few shocks of corn left in the now-harvested field. Strange. But the wheelbarrow-pusher seemed to know exactly where she was going.

Yes, it was a she, and the closer he drove the clearer it became that Dana was now pulling things out of the wheelbarrow, setting them out on the ground . . . What in the world? She waved as he drove past her, combine blades kicking up corn debris. But this was the end of the row, after all. So instead of heading straight back to the barn the way he had planned, he pulled up short, shut down his machine, and hopped out to see what was going on here.

"Your dad told me where to find you," she told him, setting out plates and cups on her picnic blanket.

"What's this?" he asked.

"What's it look like? A picnic supper for the hardworking farmer."

"You didn't have to stay late at school?"

She shook her head. "Not today. I figured we could finish that conversation we were having the other night. And besides, we just had to celebrate you finishing up the harvest."

Well, he had, sure enough. The last acre had now been trimmed of its corn stalks; the final load just needed to be unloaded. Maybe a little private celebration would be in order.

"I just want to know how you timed it so well," he said. "You been stalking me?"

She giggled. "No pun intended, right? Now how about some hot soup?"

Actually, that sounded perfect on a day like today, when October seemed to get serious again about being blustery and gray, and the clouds overhead looked pregnant with rain. The only question was, how soon would it let loose?

Snug in her scarf and bright blue sweater, Dana poured steaming tomato soup into two mugs and brought out pieces of fried chicken.

She has to know what I wanted to ask her the other night, he thought. Maybe this was her way of helping him by meeting him halfway. If so, she really knew how to make things right, and he loved her for it all the more. Even so, this was not the way the book said to do it. But he looked into her eyes as he found a place to sit on his side of the blanket.

"You want me to give thanks?" he asked. Dana nodded so he closed his eyes to pray.

"Father, thanks for this food," he began, "and for . . ."

He would have continued if it wasn't for the audible *splat* on the red-and-white-checked plastic tablecloth. He paused and went on.

"... and for the chance we have to be here, and ..."

Another splat interrupted his prayer once again; then, without further warning, a chorus of raindrops dumped on them from straight overhead.

"Oh, wow." Pete cut his prayer short with a hurried "Amen," while Dana looked up with wide eyes.

"I can't believe it," she said, wiping the rain from her face. "It wasn't supposed to rain until tonight."

So much for weather predictions. By that time—literally within seconds—the clouds had completely opened up.

"You grab the food," said Pete, scrambling to his feet. "I'll get the tablecloth."

"But—" Dana still looked as if she didn't quite believe the suddenness of the rain.

"The cab of the combine!" he yelled over a clap of thunder.

And then all he could do was help her up into the little cab, which was really only made for one person to sit in. Still they crowded inside, holding the food on their laps. And they laughed until their sides hurt.

"Want me to turn on the windshield wiper?" he asked, choking a little on a bite of chicken.

"Doesn't matter."

"Good. It stopped working ten years ago."

So they had to laugh all over again—at how silly and wet they looked, crammed into the little cab of the ancient combine. They had to laugh at the pounding rain outside, and at their ruined picnic dinner.

Well, Pete didn't call it ruined, exactly. The company was good, and he didn't mind sitting so close that they bumped elbows and had no difficulty touching noses.

"I'm so sorry," she finally told him, finishing up what was left of her soup. "I should have known this was coming."

"No apologies needed, ma'am." He finished his last piece of chicken, licked his fingers, and brought the combine to life. From now on they would need to yell to make themselves heard. "But maybe we should head back to the barn."

"What's that?" Dana cupped a hand to her ear.

"The barn!" Pete pointed out the building looming in the distance through their rain-splattered windshield. Good thing the gully-washer didn't last long; as they bumped over the rise toward the barn already it had begun to taper off.

And by the time they reached the barn and parked the combine under the lean-to roof, the downpour had diminished to a sprinkle—hardly anything to write home about.

"Well, that was a disaster," said Dana as they unloaded themselves and their soggy picnic remains from the cab.

"No, it wasn't." Pete shook his head and helped her step down. "It was, uh . . ."

"A disaster!" She finished his sentence with a laugh. "It's all right to say so."

"Well, I don't know. I don't consider dinner with you a disaster, no matter where we eat it."

She laughed again and held on to his hand.

"You always know what to say, farmer boy."

If only she knew how badly he had blown it. How he had let yet one more opportunity slip through his fingers, and how he could have kicked himself for it. No skywriting proposal, no football stadium proposal. No nothing. For a moment he thought of forgetting the whole thing, or at least going back to the proverbial drawing board. After all, if he was going to propose, he needed to do it with a little class.

What is wrong with me? he wondered. *Every chance I get, I miss!*

"Pete, are you all right?" Dana paused with a hand on his shoulder. He hadn't realized he'd been shaking. "You must be cold."

"No, it's not that. It's not that at all."

A pair of pigeons cooed far above their heads in the rafters.

"Then what?" Her voice softened as she slipped her arms around him. He took a deep breath.

"Dana, listen. Please don't say anything, I mean, not yet, because if you do I might not be able to get through this. I don't want to blow it this time."

"Okay." She pulled away a bit to get a better look at him in the dim, filtered light. But he didn't let go, and he didn't stop. "But are you sure—"

"No, please just listen. I've been trying to get up enough nerve for a long time, and if I don't say it now, I may never. In fact, I . . . I'm really not sure if I have a right to ask you this."

Her face wrinkled in a question, and she opened her mouth but said nothing.

"Dana, sometimes I think we live in different worlds, and I wonder sometimes if you could ever . . ."

No, that's not what he wanted to say. No more negative

approach. He took a deep breath and regrouped.

"Okay, forget I said that." Now he turned and faced her straight on, his hands on her shoulders. "Here's what I've been wanting to say. Dana Simons, I have loved you ever since you bumped into me in the hallway when we were in the tenth grade and I dropped all my books. I loved you when we dated in high school, and I loved you when you went away to college. And now . . . I'm not sure how it could all work, but I can't think of anyone else I want to spend the rest of my life with, so will you—"

"Yes."

Pete practically choked as she looked straight into his eyes and nodded.

"What do you mean, yes? You mean yes, you hear what I'm saying, because shoot, this isn't coming out the way I practiced. Or yes—"

"I mean yes, I will marry you, Pete."

"Oh. 'Cause you don't have to say yes right away, I mean, if you need to think about it. Or, like, pray about it. You know."

"I know. I've thought about it. I've prayed about it. And yes. If you're asking, that is. Are you asking?"

"Well, sure I'm asking. Maybe it doesn't sound like it, but I'm asking."

"And I'm saying yes. Yes, yes, yes!"

"Guess that's your final answer?"

"Will you quit it? That's my final answer!"

Actually, her kiss was the final answer, but a moment later Pete nearly choked when he remembered, and he reached into his pocket. "I can't believe it!"

"What, that you finally asked me to marry you? I've been waiting for months and months, you know. I thought for sure you would ask me last Saturday night. And then nothing happened Sunday, or Monday, or Tuesday. I figured maybe you could just use a little extra help."

"Yeah, sorry about that. I'm a little slow. Only that's not what I'm talking about." He pulled out the ring box—a little dusty around the edges but none the worse for the wear. "See, I've been carrying this around for a while. A few weeks, anyway. I read a whole stupid book about how I was supposed to propose, but none of it was any good. Here's how I was planning to do it. Actually not here in the barn, but this'll have to do."

"Here in the barn works for me."

So right there in the straw, Pete dropped to one knee just the way he'd practiced over and over in his apartment. As he did, he snapped open the ring case and presented it to Dana.

"Now, let me try it again," he said. "Dana Simons, will you marry me?"

She caught her breath as she stared at the ring Pete had bought for her; it sparkled in the dim light.

"Oh, it's beautiful."

"Put it on. The lady told me they can size it, no problem. Does it fit?"

Well, it did, or pretty close. And as Pete stood there in the barn, trying not to hyperventilate, he thought maybe he had just witnessed a miracle.

Had Dana Simons really just accepted his proposal of marriage?

Chapter Twenty-Six

Charlotte pulled a pan of steaming cornbread out of the oven for Thursday supper, which she knew would go perfectly with the hearty bowls of chili she'd just dished up.

"*Mmm.*" Bob took an appreciative whiff and wafted a bit of aroma his way with a wave of his hand. "Just the way I like it."

Better that she didn't tell him it was vegetarian chili. But he couldn't complain. And with everyone gathered at the table, along with Dana, did it get any better than this?

Actually, Charlotte was so pleased to see Dana there tonight; she was usually too busy preparing for class or working on something else for school. And Sam's regular soccer practice had been canceled for some reason. Bob sat to Charlotte's right, and offered a very nice prayer of thanks.

"Amen!" said Pete, looking up and tucking a napkin between the buttons of his plaid work shirt. Dana reached over and discreetly plucked it out of his shirt before dropping it in his lap while Charlotte stifled a smile.

That girl's taking good care of him, she thought as they passed around the cornbread and the honey. But when they reached Christopher he looked around at the table, as if he had something to say. "Did you hear about my pumpkin, Miss Simons?" he asked.

"Actually, yes." She brightened. "Your Uncle Pete told me a little. But why don't you fill me in?"

"Third place." He beamed. "Twenty bucks. And Mr. Barnes said mine should have won first for being so ugly too, except they didn't have a prize for that."

"That's wonderful," she told him, her smile matching his. "I hear you worked very hard on that project."

"Yeah. Grandpa helped me. I thought a few months ago that all my plants were going to die, but I think God made it rain at just the right times, and it ended up growing really good. And I'm going to put part of the prize in the offering plate at church. That was my deal with Grandpa."

"And with God too, huh?" Sam put in.

The adults around him chuckled, though the expression on Christopher's face made it plain he had no idea what was so funny.

Now that there was a break in the conversation, Pete cleared his throat and everyone turned in his direction. "Actually, I kind of have an announcement to make too."

Charlotte couldn't quite tell what was going on now, just that Pete suddenly looked to her a whole lot more nervous than he should have.

"So anyway," Pete went on, "what I'm trying to say here is that I asked Dana to marry me yesterday, and she said yes. We haven't set a date yet."

Oh, my! The words echoed for a moment in the kitchen before Emily screamed, Sam applauded, and Christopher shook his head and said, "Whoa." All Charlotte could think to do was get up and envelop Dana and Pete in a big group hug.

"We're so happy for you," she managed to whisper in Dana's ear, though she still had her younger son to scold.

"Why didn't you *tell* me? All day today? And you just pretended as if nothing—"

"Mom! We just wanted to announce it at the right time," he explained with a shrug, though that hardly seemed a reasonable explanation. By this time Emily was sort of hopping up and down.

"So this means I get a new aunt?" she wanted to know.

Dana wiped a happy tear and nodded. "You get a new aunt," she replied, "and I get a new niece. Pretty cool, huh?"

In fact, it was pretty cool. And who could blame Charlotte now for not being able to concentrate on the rest of the meal as they talked about wedding rings and dresses, where to hold the ceremony and who might be invited . . . So many things to plan!

Chapter Twenty-Seven

Bob had been right about one thing, as far as Charlotte could tell. He was back to doing his normal chores in a day or two. In fact, just three days later—by Friday after dinner—he sat in his favorite recliner behind that week's *Bedford Leader*, grumbling about grain prices and what the city council was up to. Just like always.

"Dear, did you hear about Emily's project?" she asked him. He had not. "The teacher said it was the best presentation she'd seen all year."

"You get your photos back?"

She frowned. "Yes, dear, I did."

"You thought they were lost."

"They were, but a Good Samaritan found them and returned them to her."

"Well, why didn't she explain about this award at dinner?" he asked, finally lowering the paper.

"She told me after school. I told her to tell you, but she said you already have enough on your mind."

"Oh." He sighed. "She should have told me anyway. She's good at that kind of thing, just like her mom was. She's a communicator. Unlike her grandpa."

"Don't say that, Bob."

"No? Why not?" He tossed the newspaper aside and shook his head in frustration. "Look at this. I've been thinking about it for days, and now it's the night before the seminar, and I still can't come up with anything."

Charlotte hadn't wanted to say anything. But to prove his point Bob snatched up a yellow pad from the magazine table next to the chair, holding it up to reveal what she assumed was a scribbled mess of speaking notes for the seminar. Charlotte wasn't sure when he'd been working on them, but at least he'd been trying.

"It's not because your eyes are still bothering you, is it?"

"No, that's not it."

"Then—"

"Eyes are good; eyes are fine," he mumbled, scribbling out the last line he'd written before tearing the whole sheet off and crumpling it into a ball. "Better than they have been in a long time. Just this stuff, it's hard to put our marriage into words."

Just then Pete poked his head in from the living room.

"How's the great American novel coming, Dad? Gonna be ready for tomorrow?"

Bob scowled as he pointed his well-chewed pencil in Pete's direction.

"You want to take a crack at this, pal?"

Pete backed away.

"Don't look at me, Dad. I'm not the one who volunteered to speak in front of dozens of—"

"Thanks for your help, Pete." Charlotte interrupted him. "If you have any ideas, you can let us know."

"Sometimes I wonder about that boy," Bob mumbled under his breath after Pete had left the room. "Dana's going to have her hands full; that's for sure."

"Shh, Bob. Don't say that."

Yes, but then what *should* he say? After another half hour, they were surely going nowhere in their brainstorming session. It didn't help to move out to the kitchen table either. Bob just sighed, winced, and wrinkled his forehead in concentration as he started over once more on his outline.

Maybe we just need more practice at this sort of thing, she told herself, and it turned into a prayer. *Lord, what are we going to do?*

But this time Bob snapped the pencil in half and looked up at her with real pain in his eyes.

"Look, Char, I'm really sorry." She didn't doubt for a moment how much he meant it. "I know I said I'd do this, but I just don't know if I'm cut out for it. I'm telling you, I have no idea what to say to those people. Give me a plow or a welder. I'll plant it, I'll build it, I'll fix it. Anything around the farm, you know I'll make it happen. But this, I just don't think I can."

For a long moment they just stared at each other, and the only sound was the ticking of the kitchen wall clock. It did Charlotte no good to see the utter helplessness in her husband's gray eyes; it reminded her of the way he looked when Dr. Carr first told him he had diabetes. She had prayed so hard back then as well.

"I'm sorry, dear." She could think of nothing else to say until they heard the sound of feet padding down the stairs.

"Grandma, do you know where the tissue—?" Emily looked around the corner but pulled up short when she saw them talking. "Oh, I'm sorry. It's nothing. I'll ask you later."

"No, wait a minute." Bob called her back. "Grandma tells me you did really well on your project. You should have told us."

"Oh." Emily looked at her slippers. "It was no big deal. I did okay."

"Okay? Best project the teacher's ever seen, and that's just 'okay'?" Bob sat back in his chair. "I don't call that just 'okay.'"

"Well." She studied her fuzzy slippers and backed up the stairs again. "I had some good photos to work with. If you start out with good stories, I guess it just kind of takes care of itself."

Bob chewed his pencil some more and seemed to think about that. *Good stories?*

And then Charlotte knew what they had to do—but not why. She looked at her watch and pushed her chair back. If this were like any other evening—and she had no reason to believe it was not—Greta would still be by her husband's bedside for the next two or even three hours. Bob looked up at her with a question.

"Where are you going?" he asked.

"It won't take long." She reached for her purse on the kitchen counter. "But please, dear. You need to come with me."

Still he didn't understand, and how could he? The problem was, Charlotte didn't quite know how to explain something she didn't quite understand herself. All she knew was where they had to go.

"Please," she said once more. "I guess you have to trust me on this one."

TO BOB'S CREDIT, he did trust his wife. She knew that he did, or at least he did come along to the Bedford Gardens Convalescent Center to visit Greta and Bud. A little tentatively at first, but he did follow Charlotte into the Alzheimer's ward and down the hall to Bud Harbinger's room.

"Knock-knock," said Charlotte.

Just as Charlotte had predicted, Greta was sitting quietly in her usual place, knitting, while Bud watched an episode of the *Jeopardy* game show on his small television. Greta looked up with a smile the moment they walked in.

"What a nice surprise!" She set down her knitting. "And . . . Bob too!"

Bob looked at the floor for a moment with his characteristic shyness before saying anything. "She needed a chauffeur this time, I guess."

Meanwhile Bud was still engrossed in his TV show, and they all paused for a moment to see what had so caught his interest.

"Car talk for four hundred," said the host, explaining something Charlotte missed about an engine.

"What is an oil filter?" said Bud, never taking his eyes off the screen, just moments before one of the TV contestants echoed the same words.

"Correct!" answered the host, but Bud didn't react.

"Bud, we have guests," Greta told her husband. "We should turn off the TV for now."

"We can come back later." Charlotte backed toward the door, but Greta would have none of it.

"Of course not. Here, let me turn that off." She reached for the remote and did it herself. Bud didn't seem to notice until Bob sat down on the edge of the bed and offered his hand.

"Good to see you again, Bud. Been a few years, hasn't it?"

Bud didn't answer but took Bob's hand with a bit of a puzzled expression.

"Bob Stevenson," said Bob. "You used to work on my equipment?"

Still Bud didn't answer, but Bob went on. "Gotta say, I miss having you around. Those younger guys, they're okay, but they don't know my old machines the way you do. Maybe you ought to come out to my place sometime, take a look at the combine. Been making a funny noise. Bet you'd be able to figure it out."

Bud took it all in quietly, even nodding slightly. Did he understand any of it? The room fell to silence.

"It was nice that you came," said Greta. "I heard you two are going to help with the young people at your church. Is that this weekend?"

"Actually, that's why we came tonight." Charlotte rearranged daisies in Greta's vase that didn't really need arranging. It gave her something to do with her hands. "We were sort of searching for a little inspiration. And I wonder if you might tell me again—tell us, I mean—the story of how you and Bud met?"

"You're sure you want to hear it all again?"

"Please. Would you be so kind? I know Bob would like to hear it."

"Well, then. You promise to stop me when it gets too boring."

Greta smiled as she picked up her knitting and recalled the story once again, how the kindly young American army sergeant from Nebraska had taken a special interest in them.

"I knew from the first time I saw him," she said, a smile playing on her lips. "From the first time when he fumbled with his little German phrase book, bringing us candy bars. I was only seventeen, but I knew it from the start."

Bob hung onto every word as she went on to explain how they came to America, the difficult adjustment for her in a strange land, leaving her parents in Berlin, the terrible accident that caused Bud to lose two fingers, and even worse, the loss of their first child who had been born prematurely in an army hospital. It had not been an easy life by any means. And Bob just shook his head, wide-eyed.

"I've never heard all these stories," he whispered quietly. "Lived here all my life, and I never heard them until now. What was I, blind?"

"Of course not." Greta smiled gently as her knitting needles clacked quietly. "Bud never wanted people to feel sorry for us. And you know we never attended the same church as you."

All true.

As Greta told her stories, Bud seemed to listen just as intently. He even reached for the photo album at one point, running his fingers across the cover, though he did not open it. By the time she finished an hour later, Bob sat with tears in his eyes before excusing himself.

"Oh, but I didn't mean—" Greta was taken aback to see him get up to leave.

"No, no." He stopped in the doorway, his back to them and his hand on his forehead. "I appreciate it. You have no idea how much."

And then he slowly turned once again, holding out his hand in Bud's direction. "I'll be back, Bud. We'll be back to visit again."

Bud raised his hand a few inches, but that was all he could do before turning back to the dark window.

Chapter Twenty-Eight

The day of the couples' seminar dawned bright and crisp, with just enough sunshine to remind Charlotte of the summer that had been, and just enough frost on the fields to give a clear preview of the winter to come.

At the moment Charlotte just hoped she looked more put together than she felt. The three chairs at the front of the church's multipurpose room faced all the others—at least fifty, in any case. Beside the chairs was a podium with a microphone. Bob fidgeted nervously from where they stood in the corner, picking at his thumbnail.

I hope he doesn't do that in front of everyone, she thought.

Still the room continued to fill with young couples. Many she recognized as friends of Pete's from school, but others...

She leaned to her left to whisper in Pastor Evans's ear.

"Who are all these people?" she asked. "I've never seen half of them."

"Must be from the Harding churches," replied the pastor. "We publicized the event up there too."

Pastor Evans looked pleased as he moved off to introduce himself to yet another young couple. Meanwhile Charlotte and Bob busied themselves by getting coffee as other couples continued to filter in. By now the room—normally used for Sunday school and church socials—was nearly packed.

"I gave up counting," Bob told her, stirring creamer into his coffee. Bob didn't take creamer. "They just keep coming."

She gently rubbed his tense shoulder and tried to set him at ease. Given the butterflies in her own stomach, that was easier said than done.

"Just remember what we talked about the other night," she reminded him. "And remember that I believe in you, no matter what."

He nodded and held up the wrinkled notes he was carrying in his fist. For the next several minutes they hunkered down in the far corner of the room, Bob crossing and uncrossing his arms and Charlotte sipping her coffee, as they waited for Pastor Evans to bring the session to order.

In time Charlotte did notice Jessica, the aide from the rest home who made the popcorn, and a young man whom Charlotte presumed was her fiancé. From across the room they didn't see her, though. Bob checked his watch yet another time.

"'Bout time to begin," he whispered. "Don't you think?"

Finally Pastor Evans launched into announcements about the couples' workbook they would hand out, childcare, their schedule for the day, and how the restrooms were right down the hall. Charlotte noticed Bob taking deep breaths.

"Don't hyperventilate," she whispered to him. "You can do it. I know you can."

"You seen Pete and Dana?" he asked back. Charlotte had not, but that didn't mean much. Pete could arrive right at zero hour, as he often did. If that was the case this morning, he and Dana might have already slipped in quietly and blended into the crowd.

In any case, Pastor Evans finished with his opening prayer, and Charlotte realized it was their turn already.

"We want to hit the ground running this morning with a special panel discussion," he said in his best emcee voice. "We've chosen a wonderful couple many of you know well. For those of you who don't, you're in for a treat."

By now Charlotte felt like fading back into the wall, but that didn't stop the introduction.

"They've been faithful members of this congregation for many years, and they're looked up to as an example of a successful partnership. So I've asked them to come share some of their secrets, and then after they've done that, we're going to open it up to questions before we go on to our workbook. Then we'll have the video and breakout sessions a little later. Now would you please welcome Bob and Charlotte Stevenson!"

It should not have surprised Charlotte when Bob took her hand as they marched up the aisle amid the applause. By this time, however, she wasn't sure whose hand shook more, hers or his. She decided it was better to just hang on as tightly as she could as they walked up together and sat in two chairs set up next to the podium. Pastor Evans kept his position behind the podium, off to the side.

"Bob," he said, "why don't you start out by telling us

a little about yourselves, maybe how you met, and then we can get into some of your wisdom. Charlotte, you feel free to chime in as well."

Charlotte gazed out over the assembled group of young people—eyes wide, many of them with pens poised and ready to take note of every word. She felt her palms sweating and hoped she would not have to shake too many hands afterward. Meanwhile, Bob fingered his notes for a moment before finally setting them aside on the podium next to her envelope of precious wedding photos. Good thing Emily hadn't lost them after all.

"Well, as Pastor Evans said, I'm Bob Stevenson." His voice started out a little unsteady. "And I got to tell you, at first I really didn't want to be here."

He paused at the chuckles before going on.

"I'm sure you're all nice folks. That's not it. It's just that I'm more used to being on my own out on a tractor, or in a barn cleaning stalls, rather than here in a room with everybody staring at me."

Again more chuckles gave him a chance to catch his breath. When he continued, he told them about the family farm and about meeting a young, pretty girl named Charlotte Coleman, asking her out, and then finally asking her to marry him.

"Guess we thought it was all pretty simple," he said. "But really I didn't think much about what made it all work, until now. See, last night my wife took me to visit a guy I thought I'd known pretty well. Lives in the rest home, and he's not doing too good anymore. Except for his wife, who's there for him every day, every night. She told us stories about all the tough times, and I won't repeat them here because she didn't exactly give me permission to do that. I'll just say that life wasn't easy for her. She went through stuff you couldn't imagine. And things didn't always turn out the way they'd hoped."

By then the room was eerily silent as everyone hung on Bob's words.

"They've been married now for sixty-some years. And to tell you the truth, I think they're the ones who should be up here, instead of us. But since you're stuck with us for now, let me just tell you what I learned from listening to her stories for a couple of hours."

Charlotte could see the couples in the front row leaning forward, not wanting to miss a thing.

"Here's the thing," Bob continued. "She didn't tell me about communication, or taking your wife out on dates, or respect, or whatever it is you guys are going to be talking about today."

He lifted up his notes and plopped them down on the podium again.

"Charlotte and I did talk through three or four things like that, you might want to know. But she reminded me what love really is about—that's giving. And forget about the fifty-fifty thing. Any marriage that's going to last is more like sixty-forty, or seventy-thirty. And that goes for both of you, the husband and the wife. You get what I'm saying?"

Charlotte had never felt more proud of her husband than she did at that moment, listening to him share his life and his love in front of all those people he had been so closed off from before. Leaving behind his notes, he simply laid out for them the basics of lasting relationships, using examples from the farm and even more from what Greta had told them last night. Commitment. Mutual respect. Knowing how to disagree. She caught Pastor Evans's eye, and he winked his approval. And there in the back row, Pete and Dana smiled at her as well.

Once in a while Charlotte found places to add her two cents' worth, which seemed to work out better than she'd expected. And she supposed it all made sense, though she didn't remember what she had said. When they got to the part about honoring their wedding vows, she even had a chance to show off her wedding pictures—until she realized that probably most of the people wouldn't be able to see them anyway. Never mind.

"My granddaughter Emily could have showed you these photos a lot better," she told them. "She had them scanned into a computer report for school, and we're very proud of her. But then, aren't all grandmothers proud of their granddaughters?"

Young as they were, the audience smiled back at her as if they understood. And perhaps they would someday, if they could all stay together as long as she and Bob had.

Before she realized it, forty-five minutes had gone by, and she and Bob started to take questions from the floor.

Charlotte answered as best she could, taking the lead now as Bob filled in with his more wry humor. It still amazed her how well the kids in the audience listened, and how they seemed to follow what she and Bob were saying.

"I guess it all comes down to something a good friend told me," she explained, reaching into her purse for the gift Greta had given her a couple of weeks back, the cross-stitch. She unrolled it and read the words once again.

"Love does not consist in gazing at each other," she read, "but in looking outward together in the same direction."

Perhaps those were enough words of wisdom for one morning. Charlotte couldn't add anything after that, and in fact they had run out of time.

"And with that," said Pastor Evans, "you're dismissed for a short break. Be back here in ten minutes."

Everyone in the room applauded, which flustered Bob and made him blush. Pete and Dana quickly found their way through the crowd to the front.

"So, Dad, when do you start your radio show?"

Bob looked as if he wasn't quite sure how to take that either, so Pete pointed at the notes.

"I mean, listen to you! And without notes even. I say that's pretty good."

"Pretty good." Bob stuffed the notes into the back pocket of his Sunday slacks. "But was there anything in there you could use?"

Pete paused and bit his lip, glancing quickly over at Dana before he stepped up and gave his father a big hug.

"There was, Dad. A lot. I'm proud of you."

Obviously startled at first, Bob hesitated for just a moment before he grabbed his son for a brief pat on the back.

Charlotte and Dana stepped aside and were sharing the moment when Charlotte caught sight of Greta Harbinger, standing alone by the back door.

By that time Greta had caught sight of the two women as well, and she made her way through the crowd holding a nice bouquet of red carnations. When she reached them, she held it out for Charlotte.

"I heard what you and Bob said," she said. "It was very good. It reminded me of the kinds of things Bud would say."

"Greta . . ." Charlotte didn't know how to answer, but she really didn't have to. Greta just held out the flowers for her as Bob rejoined them and stood close by.

"These are for both of you," she told them in a voice that could barely be heard above the hubbub of the crowd. "Remember what they mean, Charlotte?"

Bob looked at her with a look that said he didn't quite understand, but that was okay.

"I certainly do remember." Charlotte held them up so her husband of forty-six years could smell their wonderful sweet scent. "They remind us that God is faithful."

About the Author

Robert Elmer is the author of more than 50 books of Christian fiction and devotions for all ages. He and his wife live in a farming town in Washington state with their small dog, a malti-poo. They have three grown kids plus eight grandkids.

A Note from the Editors

We hope you enjoyed this volume in the Home to Heather Creek series, published by Guideposts. For over seventy-five years, Guideposts, a nonprofit organization, has been driven by a vision of a world filled with hope. We aspire to be the voice of a trusted friend, a friend who makes you feel more hopeful and connected.

By making a purchase from Guideposts, you join our community in touching millions of lives, inspiring them to believe that all things are possible through faith, hope, and prayer. Your continued support allows us to provide uplifting resources to those in need.

Whether through our online communities, websites, apps, or publications, we strive to inspire our audiences, bring them together, and comfort, uplift, entertain, and guide them.

To learn more, please go to guideposts.org.